WASHINGTON, D.C.

& THE POTOMAC REGION

"The Capital Region's Enterprises" by Mark H. Dorfman

Windsor Publications, Inc.
Chatsworth, California

A CONTEMPORARY PORTRAIT

WASHINGTON, D.C.

& THE POTOMAC REGION

WITH ALEXANDRIA, ARLINGTON, MONTGOMERY, FAIRFAX AND PRINCE GEORGE'S COUNTIES

BY BONNIE JACOB

WASHINGTON, D.C. & THE POTOMAC REGION
With Alexandria, Arlington, Montgomery,
Fairfax and Prince George's Counties

By Bonnie Jacab

Managing Editor: Linda J. Hreno
Senior Editor: Teri Davis Greenberg
Editor, Profiles: Jeffrey Reeves
Profiles Coordinator: Kelly Goulding
Assistant Profiles Coordinator: Keith Martin
Associate Editors, Profiles: Michael Nalick, Kevin Taylor
Proofreaders: Martha Cheresh, Lin Schonberger
Editorial Assistant, Profiles: Kimberly J. Pelletier

Designer: Ellen Ifrah
Photo Editors: Robin L. Sterling, Lisa Willinger
Production Associate: Jeffrey Scott Hayes
Art Production: Amanda J. Howard

Copyright © 1992 Windsor Publications, Inc.
All rights reserved.
Published in the United States of America, 1992
by Windsor Publications, Inc.,
21827 Nordhoff Street,
Chatsworth, CA 91311,
with support of CCA, Inc.
Elliot Martin, *Chairman of the Board and CEO*
J. Kelley Younger, *Publisher and Editor-in-Chief*
Nellie Scott, *Sales Maager*
Terry Pender, *Controller*
Printed in Hong Kong

Library of Congress Cataloging-in-Publication Data
Jacob, Bonnie, 1943-
Washington, D.C. & the Potomac region, with Alexandria,
Arlington, Montgomery, Fairfax, and Prince George's
Counties: a contemporary portrait / by Bonnie Jacob.
p. 196 cm. 25x31
"The capital region's enterprises" by
Mark Dorfman.
Includes bibliographical references.
ISBN 0-89781-430-4 : $32.95
1. Washington Region—Civilization. 2. Washington
Region—Description and travel. 3. Washington Re-
gion—Economic conditions. 4. Washington Re-
gion—Industries. I. Dorfman, Mark. II. Title: Washington,
D.C. and the Potomac region.
F201.J34   1992
975—dc20   91-35897
                                                   CIP

Preceding Page: Photo by
Joseph Sohm/Chromosohm

Right: Photo by Greg Pease

.....

To Douglas M. Kleine,

who sees the world around corners

CONTENTS

CHAIS du MARCHÉ FRANÇAIS

Boucherie Charcu...

Le MARG

FR

Downtown Georgetown is an historic district, but it's never out of fashion. Shops offer a choice of treasures, from designer fashions to vintage comic books. Photo by Greg Pease

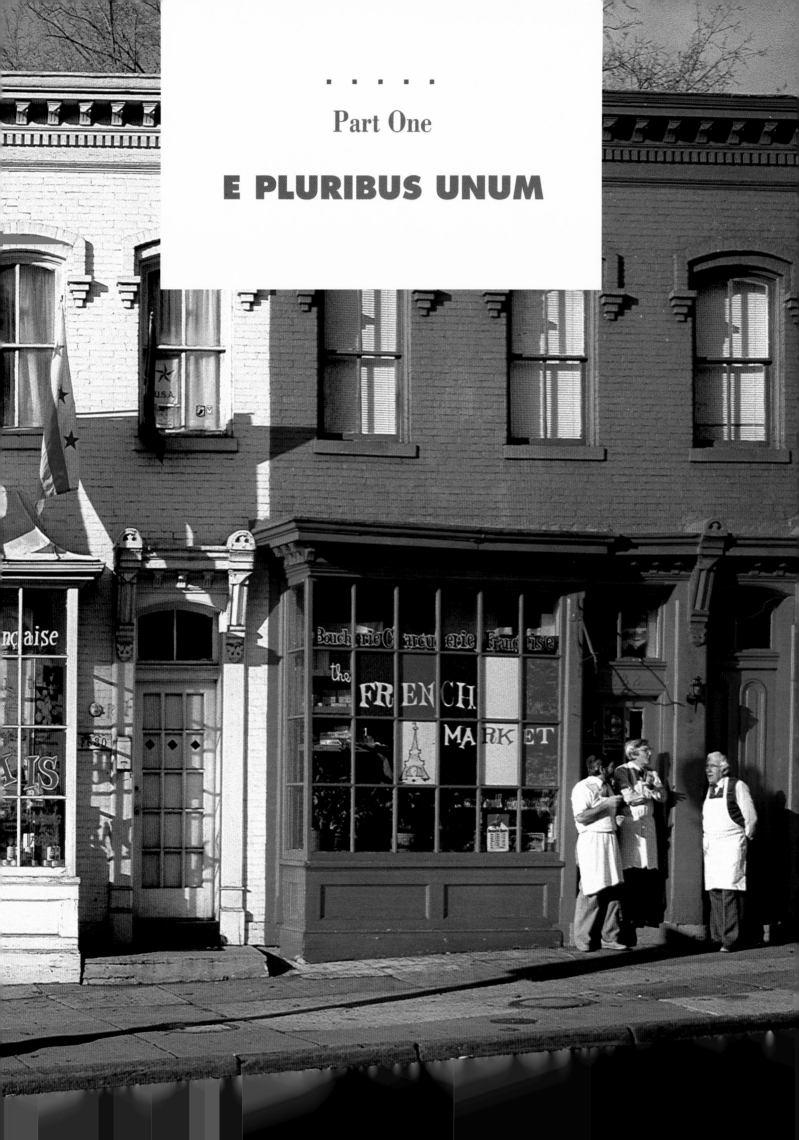

. . . . .

Part One

E PLURIBUS UNUM

INTRODUCTION

On April 15, 1791, a group of local dignitaries laid the cornerstone of a city created expressly to become the capital of the United States of America. Building a national capital from the ground up was a visionary project—many called it foolhardy—for a young country already deeply in debt, but Congress was convinced that the city ought to be fresh and independent, free from the influence of any state.

George Washington himself had picked the site for this District of Columbia: a 10-mile square of riverside bluffs and marshy plains, tobacco plantations, and family farms, which incorporated portions of Prince George's and Montgomery counties in Maryland and Fairfax County, Virginia. Two cities on the Potomac also fell within the District's boundaries—Georgetown, Maryland, and Alexandria, Virginia.

Two hundred years later Washington, D.C., remains a unique urban enterprise, a city without a state. Despite of, or perhaps, because of this circumstance, it also remains closely bound to the counties and cities whose borders originally gave way to its own.

As the District of Columbia has grown into a world center of government and commerce, its neighbors have prospered, too. In recent decades they have evolved from rural suburbs into thriving population centers with identities, economies, and even full-size downtowns of their own. The colonial city of Alexandria flourishes once more as a cosmopolitan port of call for millions of visitors as well as home to more than 200 national associations. Neighboring Arlington County maintains a luxurious balance between business growth and community life. Overlooking the Blue Ridge foothills and Dulles International Airport, fast-growing Fairfax County is the location of choice for corporate giants such as Mobil and General Dynamics. Montgomery County's fast-moving, high-tech corridor now accounts for nearly 10 percent of the nation's biomedical research, while its two dozen golf courses challenge Sunday players as well as touring pros. Prince George's County, home of Goddard Space Flight Center and the University of Maryland, draws young families to its close-knit communities and innovative public school system.

Connected by the 90-mile Metrorail rapid transit system and some 300 miles of freeways, capital-area juris-

11

dictions maintain an effective regional infrastructure through formal organizations such as the Metropolitan Washington Council of Governments. They also cooperate *ad hoc* on many shared concerns, including efforts to restore the Chesapeake Bay. Federal agencies throughout the region long ago established strong economic bonds between the District and its neighbors. Regional banks and retailers also contribute to the mutual economic base. Citizens keep in touch across state and county lines through areawide coverage by newspapers and television stations. Sports fans cheer the Redskins football team, which trains in Virginia and plays in the District, as well as the Prince George's-based Washington Bullets basketball and Capitals hockey teams.

The capital region today is home to more than 3 million people who enjoy its hilltop vistas and riverfront parks, its music and museums, its colleges, its sports teams, its affluence. National leaders and average citizens move here for their tours of duty and remain for lifetimes, sharing quiet, hometown neighborhoods with diplomats, world business and financial moguls, famous writers, top doctors, scientists, educators, and lawyers, and

the nation's highest concentration of brainy "Jeopardy" champions.

As a place to work, the area offers unparalleled excitement and rewards. The political capital of the ever-expanding free world, it is also a center of finance, telecommunications, and high-technology industries. Its work force leads the nation in white-collar jobs, working women, minority enterprise, and average household income.

As Washington, D.C., moves into its third century, its metropolitan reach continues to expand outward. More than 100,000 workers now commute here from as far away as Pennsylvania and West Virginia. Regional businesses, looking toward the day when Washington and Baltimore merge into a statistical metropolis, are already promoting the area as a "Common Market."

At the heart of it all, Washington, D.C., remains the proud seat of government and symbolic hometown for the residents of each of the 50 states. Leading the grand tradition of American enterprise, the city is a splendid monument to people with the vision to see a nation's capital on the muddy banks of the Potomac River—and the courage to build it.

Photo by Walter Larrimore

Chapter One

WASHINGTON, D.C.

∎ ∎

A City Comes of Age

Seeing the United States Capitol for the first time, children often react as if they were meeting a celebrity. Some point at it, confident and familiar. Others get unexpected fits of the giggles. Maybe they hesitate just for an instant while they compare the images remembered from TV news with the grand, white structure that looms before their eyes. Is it bigger than they expected? Smaller? Most of the time they decide that it's pretty exciting, no matter what. Then they snap its picture.

Shown proudly to the folks back home, schoolchildren's snapshots, like the pictures on the news and the photos in travel magazines, keep the monuments and public buildings of Washington, D.C., before the eyes of America and the world. They are indeed old friends: the White House, with its thrusting porticos and wide, green lawns; the Lincoln Memorial, with its gentle, giant sculpture of the seated President; the Jefferson Memorial, serene above the Tidal Basin, surrounded by thousands of cherry trees; the Vietnam Memorial, with 58,183 names of lost soldiers inscribed in a long, black wall; the Washington Monument on the Mall, crowned by flags and fireworks on the Fourth of July.

These images are well worth framing, especially at night, when pale marble pediments and granite columns on Capitol Hill and the Mall below are transformed into an ancient city bathed in incandescent light. Still, this

Thanks to countless bake sales and car washes back home, high school bands from across the United States perform proudly in capital parades and celebrations. Units from capital region schools also rank among the nation's best. Photo by Greg Pease

12

Washington, D.C., of travelogues and calendars is only one face of the capital city, which more than 609,000 people call home. Among the parks and monuments exists a vigorous and modern American city whose daily business is the business of the world.

Like many great cities, the District is a congregation of small towns that share streets, subways, and newspapers, and cross paths at Redskins football games. Each of these communities contributes a distinctive definition of the "real" Washington, D.C.

It is, of course, the home of the capital of the United States and the reason why the District of Columbia was established here on the marshy banks of the Potomac 200 years ago. In addition to housing the President, Congress, and the Supreme Court, the city is headquarters for the hundreds of agencies and various military facilities that serve them. These agencies are staffed by more than 200,000 clerks, specialists, managers, and administrators who flood into federal offices from the city's residential neighborhoods and suburbs every working day.

The presence of the federal government has made Washington, D.C., a magnet for the people and institutions who want to do business with it, influence it, or otherwise catch its eyes and ears. Likewise, it is a prime beat for thousands of newspapers, periodicals, newsletters, broadcast and cable networks, free-lance writers, and elec-

tronic information services that carry news of government activities to the nation and the world.

As the nation's capital, Washington, D.C., has also evolved into a showplace for its treasures. The Smithsonian Institution owns more than 100 million works of art, artifacts, and natural wonders; the sampling offered by its 13 museums ranges from the Air & Space Museum's moon rocks to the Museum of Natural History's Hope Diamond. The Library of Congress holds more than 400 million publications, photographs, films, recordings, vintage advertisements, and musical instruments.

Just around the corner from the Library of Congress, the privately owned Folger Shakespeare Library owns 79 of the 240 First Folios (1623) of the Bard's work known to exist. The Phillips Collection, The Corcoran Gallery of Art, and at least three dozen other nongovernment museums around the city showcase works by Renoir, Jasper Johns, and Goya, Navajo textiles, Afro-American history, pre-Columbian art, artifacts of the women's suffrage movement, those

From the National Press Club downtown, Washington correspondents speed news from the White House and Capitol Hill to media worldwide. Photo by Greg Pease

America's most recognized symbol, the present U.S. Capitol dome was completed in 1863. President Abraham Lincoln kept construction going during the Civil War as a signal that the Union would continue. Photo by Joseph Sohm/Chromosohm

of great naval battles, and children's sculptures.

Many of Washington's buildings are works of art themselves, the crowning achievements of leading architects from many eras. Benjamin Latrobe, the city's first great architect, designed the main gate of the Navy Yard; and William Thornton created the fine Federal-style Octagon House as well as the prizewinning design for the Capitol. James Renwick designed the Gothic, red sandstone castle for the Smithsonian Institution's headquarters; and Adolph Cluss created the robust Victorian Arts and Industries building for the Smithsonian.

Along D.C. streets students of architecture will spot a virtual history of design styles: Smithmeyer's and Pelz's Italian Renaissance Jefferson Building for the Library of Congress; Montgomery Meigs' Italian Victorian Old Pension Building; Daniel Burnham's Beaux Arts Union Station; Paul Cret's classical deco Folger Library; John Russell Pope's classical revival National Archives; Marcel Breuer's "Brutalist" Department of Housing and Urban Development Build-

ing; I. M. Pei's angular modern National Gallery East Building; Arthur Cotton Moore's postmodern Washington Harbour; and Arthur Erickson's neo-neo-classical Embassy of Canada.

Gardens great and small soften the cityscape and delight the eye. Frederick Law Olmsted designed the lawns and flower beds that skirt the Capitol; Beatrix Farrand envisioned the 10 acres of formal gardens, fountains, pools, wooded nooks, and pathways lavished about the Dumbarton Oaks mansion in Georgetown. Visitors love to photograph the colorful summertime display of marigolds, zinnias, Indian paintbrush, and other backyard favorites in the "Annual Library" planted by the U.S. National Park Service near the Tidal Basin and the Victorian profusion of violet and white cabbage roses in the Enid A. Haupt Garden in front of the Smithsonian Castle. Constitution Gardens, created to complement the Mall for the U.S. Bicentennial, is a fitting showplace for a growing collection of memorials. The Mall itself, casual and sometimes muddy, is a place that welcomes play.

Daniel Chester French's giant sculpture of the seated President in the Lincoln Memorial is one of the city's most beloved sights. Shadows on the face cause its expression to shift with the changing light. Photo by Greg Pease

The Lincoln Memorial was completed in 1929. Thin marble panels in the ceiling above the statue were treated with beeswax so that sunlight would glow through. Courtesy, National Archives

Washington is also home to landmark churches representing many of the world's religions: the recently completed gothic Cathedral Church of Saints Peter and Paul (National Cathedral) is a masterpiece of handmade stained-glass windows and handcarved gargoyles; the massive Roman Catholic National Shrine of the Immaculate Conception is awesome for its splendid mosaics. The Islamic Center is a treasure of Middle Eastern art and carpets. The nation's largest Greek Orthodox congregation meets under the Byzantine arches and mosaics of Santa Sophia. Afro-Americans gather at the historic Metropolitan A.M.E. church, home church of presidential advisor Frederick Douglass. Every President since James Madison has attended services at Benjamin Latrobe's exquisite cream and white St. John's Church, just across from the White House on Lafayette Square.

Of course, having the federal government as a neighbor gives Washingtonians a unique perspective on the democratic process. They can watch a law being debated on the floors of Congress or watch lobbyists schmooze with legislators at power breakfasts in the English Grill at the Hay Adams Hotel or the coffee shop at the Mayflower. They can sit in the Supreme Court chamber to hear decisions being read and debate them later in the court cafeteria. They can crowd onto the fringes of the Capitol grounds to see the President being inaugurated or pick a spot along Pennsylvania Avenue to watch the parade. If scandal breaks out—as it surely will—they can read all about it in the *Washington Post.*

All Washingtonians are *de facto* insiders. They spot their neighbors on the covers of *Newsweek* and *Time* and try to see how many players they can recog-

an exciting international city as well. Almost 150 nations have embassies or legations here. The city is also home to headquarters of worldwide organizations such as the International Red Cross and the Organization of American States as well as institutions for world finance, communications, and trade.

This international community offers the city daily opportunities for cross-cultural experiences such as film showings at the embassy of France or fashion shows sponsored by Spain or Italy. The People's Republic of China imported a team of cooks from the mainland to operate a restaurant that set a new standard for local Chinese cuisine for

nize without a scorecard each summer at charity games starring congressional softball teams. They know where to spot the movie stars who routinely drop into town to testify before Congress or lead a demonstration for a favorite cause. They can arrange a VIP tour of the White House or the FBI for visiting relatives. Those really in the know swear they can spot an international crisis brewing when White House staffers begin ordering late-night dinners from the pizza franchise down the street. During the Desert Storm war, it is said, orders delivered to the White House jumped to 50 pizzas a night.

As the capital of the ever-widening free world, Washington has evolved into

several years. The wife of a recent British ambassador became honorary patron to the area's blossoming community theaters, and embassies often open their doors to local charities for fundraising events. Children from public and private schools in the District mingle with youngsters from other nations on special projects or field trips. Diplomats form national teams for Sunday afternoon polo matches on the Mall.

Having the world at the doorstep means occasional close encounters with world leaders. When the Queen of England or members of her family drop into town for state visits, they also call on community centers and schools; Princess Diana even found time to swim

Generations of Washingtonians and tourists have enjoyed quiet walks beneath 600 cherry trees that ring the Tidal Basin. The Japanese government donated the trees in 1912 as a gesture of friendship. Photo by Greg Pease

RICHARD L MATTHEWS
THOMAS HOPKINS · GARY W HULSE · CURTIS J KAUPP · DOUGLAS H KIKER
JOHN R MILLER · MARVIN J NASCHEK · CARMELO NAVARRO
BILLIE JOE ONTIS
WAYNE E SKOLITS · CHARLES L SMITH · JOE H STANLEY · EDDY G SUMPTER
MELVIN E THOMPSON · ANTHONY F WASHINGTON
DONALD R WENTZ · KENNETH A BAKER · GEORGE L BARNES
DAVID A CASSIDY · GREGORY B CHIAGO
GEORGE W FISH Jr · LEROY D HOFFMAN
PATRICK R HENDRICKSON · DONALD L FORD
RAYMOND B KYZER · DAVID G LENGYEL · HAROLD D MILLER
CHARLES A OLSON · RONALD J PANICCIA
RAYMOND P SANTORA · PAUL A STEIN · THOMAS E SHEPPARD
RICHARD C SWIFT
DAVID I BRIGGS
BRADLEY C CUTHBERT
DONALD L GOLDSMITH
DAVID W HEMPHILL
NOAH L SMITH
THOMAS W WARREN

some early morning laps in the pool of a local school. Heads of state enjoy *tête à tête* luncheons at Capitol Hill restaurants or slip out with but a bodyguard or two for private walks among the monuments. Former Soviet President Mikhail Gorbachev, in town for a summit conference, thrilled a rush-hour crowd of workers when he got out of his limousine at a Connecticut Avenue corner and started shaking people's hands.

Washingtonians learn not to be surprised at such goings-on, but they never become truly jaded, either. The nation's capital is, after all, a hometown at heart.

Some residents of the District of Columbia can trace their families back to English farmers and former Scottish indentured servants who owned the land here while the city gradually grew up around it. Others are the progeny of Irish laborers who also came to build the federal city. Many more are descended from the black slaves who built the White House and the Capitol or from the thousands of former slaves who began new lives in the federal city after the Civil War. Idealistic government workers journeyed here from home districts across America to be part of the New Deal, the New Frontier, the Great Society, or Reaganomics. They or their children also live here still.

Recent surges of immigration have brought large communities of Asians, Central Americans, Caribbean islanders, Arabs, and Africans into the District. They are changing the demographic profile of the city, whose black majority

now shares the city's 69 square miles with growing percentages of whites, Hispanics, and Asians. Like many of the great eastern cities, Washington has lost population to the suburbs since the 1960s; lately, though, that trend has

been slowing. Many people, including young families who have traditionally sought open suburban spaces, are moving back to the city.

The city they all share is a grand stage for everyday lives. Its skyline is lowrise; its public spaces are human scale. Residents tend their gardens and wash their cars within a glance of the Capitol dome or the spires of the National Cathedral. On their way to work, they dutifully wait at streetlights for

Presidential motorcades to pass, then continue to their own desks or workstations in some of the most powerful offices in the world. They can lunch next to a Senator at a famous restaurant or wait in line with the tourists for a half smoked hot dog or an egg roll from a street-corner cart. They can shop with the trendsetters at Yves St. Laurent's *Rive Gauche* and Chanel or pick up a bangle from one of the city's hundreds of street vendors.

They go home to neighborhoods as diverse as Washingtonians themselves. Georgetown, older than Washington by 50 years, remains lively with students and young professionals who enjoy its shops, restaurants, and nightlife, as well as the aristocrats whose showplace townhouses repose on its cobbled back streets. Capitol Hill's townhouses are popular with Congress and staffers as well as many families who have lived there for generations. Adams-Morgan is the city's most diverse neighborhood,

popular with Hispanic and Caribbean immigrants and others who enjoy its marketplace atmosphere; other Latino newcomers choose the nearby Mt. Pleasant area. Chinatown, whose giant Friendship Arch was a gift from Beijing, the District's sister city, maintains a venerable presence in rows of nineteenth-century storefronts downtown.

Many of the District's oldest black families still live in the elegant Victorian cottage-style homes in LeDroit Park or in the grand residences along the "Gold Coast" up the hill from the White House on Sixteenth Street, N.W. The beaux arts mansions and townhouses in Kalorama are homes to embassies, diplomats, and old-line Washington "cave dwellers"; other longtime residents enjoy the elegance and convenience of the great art deco apartment buildings in Woodley Heights. Families of means raise children and azaleas in the bungalows, colonials, and mansions of Friendship Heights, University Park, and Cleveland Park.

Above: The Smithsonian's Air and Space Museum offers a chance to touch a piece of the moon and to play astronaut to the heart's content. Photo by Bob Rowan/Progressive Image Photography

Facing page: The Supreme Court becomes a busy place after the annual session begins on the first Monday in October. Designed in 1935 by Cass Gilbert, the neoclassical building contains many art deco touches. Photo by Jake McGuire/Washington Stock Photo

Mansions once home to Gilded Age millionaires on Dupont Circle are now apartments for students and professors, lawyers, artists, and current millionaires; mansions farther up Massachusetts Avenue now fly the flags of the world's governments on Embassy Row. Logan Circle, once home to Mary Bethune McLeod, the famed black educator, and other civic leaders, remains a beautifully preserved neighborhood of Victorian townhouses. The Circle is part

of the revitalized Shaw district, home to many of the city's early black-owned businesses and the legendary theaters of the "great black way."

Many Victorian homes can also be found in Old Anacostia across the river from Capitol Hill. Nearby Benning Heights is a quiet, residential suburb with a bird's-eye view of the city. Trolley

suburbs Brookland and Takoma Park remain leafy, quiet, family hometowns. Deanwood, where slaves once served on a large family farm, is now a comfortable community whose middle-class black residents trace back their families in the area for generations.

Two hundred years ago the great city of Washington, D.C., consisted of a single sandstone marker. Quarried from George Washington's Aquia Creek, the stone was set in place on the jetty of land known as Jones Point in Alexandria, Virginia, on April 15, 1791, to mark the first corner on the 10-mile-square boundary of the new District of Columbia. The ceremony was conducted according to ancient masonic rites by the master of the lodge with the mayor of Alexandria, the three commissioners of the District of Columbia, other local dignitaries, and a reporter from the *Gazette* in attendance. Following the ceremony, the Reverend Mr. Muir gave a blessing, "May jealousy...be buried deep under the work which this day we have completed, brethren and gentlemen."

The new city was a creation, mainly, of politics. Unable to agree on which of them would provide a permanent home to the capital of the new United States, the 13 former colonies decided to establish an independent Federal District. Its location on the banks of the Potomac was the result of a compromise between northern and southern states masterminded by Thomas Jefferson: the South would get the honor of having the capital city and northern interests would be reimbursed for money loaned to the Continental Army during the Revolutionary War.

Shortly thereafter Congress made the agreement official in the Residence Act of 1790. It gave President George Washington the right to select the specific site for the new territory; no one was surprised when it included his hometown of Alexandria, Virginia, as well as the port city of Georgetown, Maryland, just below the Potomac fall line. Washington believed that the Potomac was the gateway to trade with the West; local residents expected a windfall of at least $100,000 per year just from having the government nearby.

To design the new capital, Washington hired Pierre L'Enfant, a young

French engineer who had served with the Continental Army during the Revolution. L'Enfant understood that his commission was both historic and unique: "No Nation had ever before offered them of deliberately deciding on the spot where their Capital City should be fixed," he had written earlier to the President. The new City of Washington was to cover only a few square miles of the District—known as the Territory of Columbia—beside the river on the Maryland side of the Potomac. This left room for growth, the designer observed.

"The plan should be drawn on such a scale as to leave room for that aggrandizement and embellishment which the increase of the wealth of the nation will permit it to pursue at any period however remote."

Drawing on boyhood memories of Versailles, L'Enfant planned a great, formal city with avenues radiating geometrically from parks and squares; broad ceremonial vistas would unite the President's House with the Capitol and the Capitol with the Potomac. Sadly the challenge of realizing his vision upon these bare, muddy fields proved too much for the temperamental artist. After waiting a year for L'Enfant to provide a working map of the new city, Washington reluctantly fired him. A local surveyor was hired to finish the job according to L'Enfant's plan. Designs for the Capitol and President's House, which L'Enfant had also promised to provide, were selected from a public competition.

From the first the new capital was swamped by financial difficulty. Still struggling with debts from the Revolutionary War, the federal government hoped to finance its public buildings by selling land donated to the government by its original owners within the District; in fact, the lots at the time were all but worthless. Unable to find or afford to hire free laborers, the government rented slaves from neighboring plantations. Slowly the first elegant structures rose from the tidal marsh. The Residence Act of 1790 had given the government 10

Formal gardens surround Georgetown's Dumbarton Oaks mansion. During World War II, J. Robert Oppenheimer met here with officials to plan the Manhattan Project, which produced the atomic bomb. Later, Allied leaders discussed peace plans here. Photo by Bob Rowan/Progressive Image Photography

years to make the capital ready; it needed every second of that just to make it habitable.

By the time the federal furniture began arriving by boat from the temporary Capitol in Philadelphia in 1800, about 3,000 people lived in the city, including farmers, slaves, tradespeople, and 137 government clerks. They lived in the fewer than 400 houses that stood within the city limits, including two boardinghouses built by George Washington to provide lodging for Congress-

men and to stimulate the economy. One wing of the Capitol was more or less complete and some the President's House was sound enough for John and Abigail Adams to take up residence. Buildings for the departments of War and Navy were finished, while those for the Treasury, State, and the Post Office were coming along.

"The President's House is in a beautiful situation in front of which is the Potomac with a view of Alexandria," Abigail Adams wrote to her sister. "The country around is romantic ... a wilderness at best."

Early Presidents and First Ladies brought sophistication to the new city. Thomas Jefferson invited a European botanist to set up a national botanical garden and 16 Italian musicians to improve the sound of the marine band. James and Dolley Madison turned the

President's House into a salon for the business leaders and intelligentsia who moved to Washington to manage federal departments. Their guest lists also included visiting Native-American chiefs from the western territories and travel writers from abroad.

When the British invaded the city in 1814 and burned most of its public buildings to the ground, Congress briefly considered moving elsewhere; local citizens hastily built a temporary red-brick Capitol and the government stayed. Still, the goals of Congress and Washingtonians were not always the same. Many congressmen objected strongly to the practice of slavery, which was still legal in the District. Alexandria, in particular, was a major center of slave trading. Washington residents, in turn, found the federal government to be an autocratic landlord. District residents were not permitted to vote in national elections, had no representation in Congress, and received no taxes from the government for public buildings and land. In 1846 disagreements over these issues of slavery and finances caused citizens of Alexandria (city and county) to ask to be returned to Virginia; Congress quickly agreed.

Surrounded by southerners, the federal government found itself a virtual outsider in its own capital during the Civil War. When the fighting began, Union troops quickly circled the city with a ring of 68 forts. Within the city rumors of spies were common, and several local ladies and gentlemen were jailed as Rebel sympathizers.

Although it was never invaded, the city suffered considerable wear and tear during the war. Homes were commandeered for Army purposes; troops and

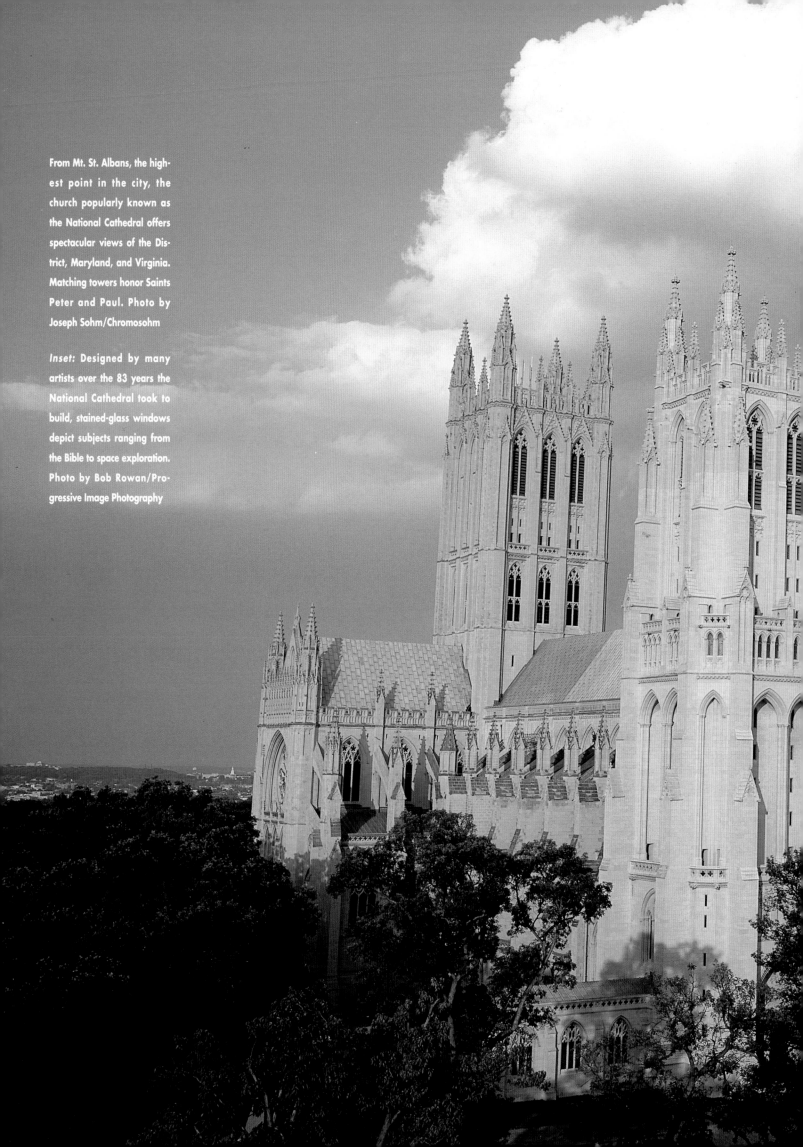

From Mt. St. Albans, the highest point in the city, the church popularly known as the National Cathedral offers spectacular views of the District, Maryland, and Virginia. Matching towers honor Saints Peter and Paul. Photo by Joseph Sohm/Chromosohm

Inset: Designed by many artists over the 83 years the National Cathedral took to build, stained-glass windows depict subjects ranging from the Bible to space exploration. Photo by Bob Rowan/Progressive Image Photography

equipment tore up the still unpaved streets. Thousands of former slaves found refuge here under the protection of the Union Army. Along with federal war workers, demobilized soldiers, and local farmers uprooted by the fighting, they swelled the population of the city from 60,000 in 1861 to more than 140,000 at war's end.

In 1871 the City of Washington, Georgetown, and surrounding county lands were united as the District of Columbia. For a few years the District was more or less self-governed as a territory. This experiment finally got the streets paved but practically bankrupted the local treasury. Still, public and private Washington began drawing closer together. Instead of living in boarding-houses and commuting to their home districts, more Senators and Representatives brought their families and established homes here. The Civil Service of 1883 replaced the patronage system with a permanent federal work force. Wealthy government dignitaries took advantage of a real estate boom to develop suburbs that pushed into rural northwest Washington and Maryland. Congress appropriated money to fill in the swampy flats along the Potomac, and, as the District's centennial approached, to extend L'Enfant's plan for the original City of Washington out to the District borders.

Entering the twentieth century, Washington began to look and feel like a world capital. Great Britain, France, and Italy replaced their legations with full-scale embassies. Visiting world leaders were entertained by Gilded Age tycoons in their mansions on Dupont and Sheridan circles. Many of the city's black residents established social and intellectual coteries in gracious neighborhoods such as Logan Circle and LeDroit Park. Senator James McMillan headed a commission to restore the Mall and other city parks to the classical symmetry envi-

sioned by its designer and encouraged other improvements inspired by the City Beautiful movement then sweeping Europe. In 1912 the Japanese government gave the city the cherry trees that now ring the Tidal Basin and other landmarks as a gesture of friendship.

World War I flooded the city with new federal workers; the population leaped from 350,000 to 526,000 between April 1917 and April 1918. Many of the newcomers migrated into the Maryland and Virginia suburbs. Others found modestly priced housing in the city's oldest neighborhoods in Georgetown and Capitol Hill, beginning the process of gentrification, which would make them fashionable once again. Thousands of idealistic young workers who arrived in the 1930s to work on New Deal social programs turned restoration into full-scale historic preservation, while giant public works projects such as the Federal Triangle

A formation of World War I Keystone Bombardment Airplanes of the 2nd Bombardment Group shows its stuff in the skies above the Capitol. The Wright Brothers tested and developed their airplane for military purposes with the army at Fort Myers in Arlington. Courtesy, National Archives

gave Pennsylvania Avenue the classical face that Thomas Jefferson had envisioned.

Overwhelming growth continued through the Second World War, finally peaking in 1950 at more than 800,000. By now the federal city had literally burst its boundaries: the Pentagon was across the river in Virginia, and the National Naval Medical Center was in Bethesda, Maryland. Ironically, as the capital grew into a regional entity, it also began looking more and more like a hometown. It had a baseball team, the Senators, and a football team, the Redskins. The Arena Stage Company, founded in 1951, attracted a resident troupe of talented actors. Cabinet officials joined local socialites on the boards of Children's Hospital and the National Symphony Orchestra. In 1961 the Twenty-third Amendment even gave District citizens the right to vote for the President and Vice President of the United States.

In the 30 years since receiving the franchise, Washington has matured as both city and symbol. A new Home Rule Charter in 1970 gave the unified District its first elected mayor and city council, along with a non-voting delegate to the House of Representatives. Guided by the Pennsylvania Avenue Development Corporation, a private organization created by Congress in 1972, the nation's "main street" has been revitalized by new construction and imaginative rehabilitation. Today it is a grand promenade for national ceremonies as well as a delightful place for an afternoon stroll. Major revitalization projects have restored pride and economic energy to other neighborhoods as well.

In 1991, on its 200th birthday, the city once known as "Congress' favored child" continues to come of age. A new municipal administration headed by Mayor Sharon Pratt Kelly has earned the respect of voters and Congress; as a result, Congress has authorized a long-term funding commitment, made in lieu of taxes on federal property, which will, for the first time, allow the city to plan its financial strategies several years ahead. Meanwhile, a newly elected "shadow" Senator and Representative lobby for a Constitutional amendment that will give the District full representation in Congress as a state.

The District of Columbia continues to struggle with an epidemic of poverty-related social problems and drug-related crimes; but it is also highly regarded for its willingness to provide compassionate social services such as shelter for the homeless and care for babies suffering from substance withdrawal and AIDS. Its programs for the elderly are among the region's best; health-care workers are untiring in their efforts to provide prenatal and postnatal care to mothers and babies.

Some of the District's 4,800-member police force give countless volunteer hours to its Boys and Girls clubs and other organizations that provide youngsters with positive role models and activities. The Department of Parks and Recreation likewise works hard at presenting imaginative programs that keep kids healthy and busy at almost 125 recreation and after-school centers.

Citizens can enjoy more than 8,200 acres of parkland, including the wild, naturally forested swath that follows Rock Creek across northwest Washington to the Potomac along with dozens of well-groomed municipal playgrounds and tennis courts.

The District boasts a half dozen major private universities, a dozen

Facing page: During World War II years, as many as 100,000 people a day, including service personnel, war workers, and visitors, passed through Washington's Union Station. Courtesy, Library of Congress, Prints and Photographs Division

Above: Marchers, hundreds of thousands strong, follow Dr. Martin Luther King, Jr., and other Civil Rights leaders to the Mall in the 1963 March on Washington for Jobs and Freedom. Courtesy, National Archives

From a terrace at George-
town's Washington Harbour,
diners have an open-air view
of the waterfront, Roosevelt Island, and the Arlington County
skyline. Photo by Carol Highsmith Photography

other institutes of higher learning, plus
an up-and-coming city university system. Of its 14 hospitals, three are teaching facilities.

About 82,000 students attend the District's 178 public schools, including
highly regarded magnet schools such as
the Duke Ellington School of the Arts.
There are almost 100 private schools
and academies as well.

Many of the city's programs are administered from its new Reeves Center;
another new municipal building is
scheduled to open in 1992. Despite the
many problems that still frustrate the

District, as they do many other cities,
Washington residents have begun to talk
confidently of the future. This is because
now, more than ever before, their future
is in their own hands.

This new era of self-determination is
particularly evident in the city's business
and economic community.

Ever the capitalist, George Washington intended for the capital to have a
broad base of commerce, but, almost
from the first, it has been a "company
town." The company, of course, has
been the federal government, whose
payroll created most of the District's

filled by the growth of local business. By almost any measure, the star of the show is MCI Communications, a *Fortune 500* company whose annual sales leaped from $144 million in 1980 to almost $7.7 billion in 1990. Two other publicly held local companies, the Washington Post Company and Potomac Electric Power Company (PEPCO), also achieved well over one billion dollars in revenues during 1990.

During the 1980s the District became increasingly attractive to national and multinational investors and retailers, whose logos and limos give the District the look of a world business capital. The city also continued to solidify its place as a center of finance as home to the World Bank, the International Monetary Fund, and the Import-Export Bank. The federally created Federal National Mortgage Association, popularly known as Fannie

wealth and whose policies determined its growth.

During the 1980s, however, the city's business profile changed dramatically. Privatization of federal programs and services slowed the growth of the government work force and encouraged private providers of computer software, social services, and an assortment of high-tech management skills. Federal agencies continued their trend, begun in the 1930s, of relocating facilities to the suburbs, further reducing the share they contribute to local earnings.

Any vacuum thus created has been

Mae, and the Student Loan Marketing Association, known as Sallie Mae, both headquartered in the city, saw their combined assets grow to a total of $175 billion. One of Washington's oldest local financial institutions, Riggs National Bank, closed out 1990 with more than $7 billion in assets.

Although its economic center of gravity has shifted from the public to the private sector, Washington's principal product is the same as it was 200 years ago: paperwork. The city boasts the largest per capita concentration of lawyers in the United States, including

A Latin-American festival in Adams-Morgan brings out a youthful and appreciative crowd. Photo by Larry Ghiorsi/ Brooklyn Image Group

almost a quarter of the 100 attorneys listed by *American Lawyer* magazine as the nation's most influential. The granite-and-glass office buildings along the downtown power corridors also contain the fax machines of hundreds of lobbyists and public relations specialists, as well as many of the more than 2,200 national trade and professional associations that have offices in the city. Policy research groups (think tanks) and public interest advocacy groups ruminate in

ornate Victorian brownstones near Dupont Circle or in restored Federal-style townhouses on Capitol Hill. Not surprisingly this city of documents also supports the nation's highest per capita concentration of bicycle couriers.

Every Washingtonian who has ever been engulfed by a sixth-grade class from Ohio would agree that tourism is the city's most visible industry. The nation's fifth most popular tourist destination, Washington earns the lion's share of more than $7.6 billion spent in the region annually by sightseers and business travelers. During the 1980s a giant new convention center in the heart of downtown made it possible for the city to handle most large-scale events. The center's presence has since been a catalyst for the revitalization of surrounding commercial blocks.

Not surprisingly, Washington's residents compare impressively with those of other major cities in terms of household income and education. More than 84 percent of its civilian labor force of 337,000 was employed in white-collar fields as of 1990. The Washington work force includes one of the highest percentages of working women of any city, and the District's percentage of minority-owned business ranks number three

among the nation's cities. Despite a mild recession—a rarity in this city, which has traditionally been considered recession proof—local unemployment experienced a net drop in the last decade.

During the 1980s Washington's own local cultural scene has flourished as well. Theater patrons have a choice unrivaled outside of New York. The Arena Stage Company is now the centerpiece of a fertile resident theater community that includes more than a dozen producing companies at any time, including Wooly Mammoth, Studio, and The Source theater companies. The main stages of the John F. Kennedy Center for the Performing Arts and the National Theater host blockbuster touring shows and original productions. The Shakespeare Theatre at the Folger presents classic and contemporary plays to full houses in a richly carved replica of an Elizabethan playhouse. Future stars of stage and television continue to be trained at Catholic

University's Hartke Theatre. Excellence on local stages is recognized by the Helen Hayes Award, named for one of the city's most eminent daughters.

Legendary jazz musician and composer Duke Ellington was also born in Washington, D.C., and, he, too, has his legacy. The Duke Ellington School of the Arts, part of the D.C. public school system, is an important training stage for young artists. Other musicians follow in the footsteps of Capitol Hill's John Philip Sousa and hone their skills in oompah marches as well as jazz, blue grass, chamber music, and symphony orchestral performance with one of the many military musical groups stationed in the area. At least a generation of folk musicians has found kindred audiences in

the clubs and in the grassy park around Dupont Circle.

Under the direction of the great Russian cellist Mstislav Rostropovich, the National Symphony Orchestra, founded in 1931, has achieved international stature. Similarly, the Washington Opera, the Washington Ballet, and the Paul Hill Chorale have all transcended their origins as local companies.

Founded in 1888, the Corcoran School of Art has encouraged generations of painters, sculptors, and photographers; local painters led by Gene Davis created the important contemporary abstract art movement known as the Washington Color School. Lois Maillou Jones, the painter whose pioneering representation of Afro-American themes and people in fine art grew out of the Harlem Renaissance in the 1920s, is a professor at Howard University.

Even before Librarian of Congress and poet Archibald MacLeish opened the library to the public in 1940s, federal institutions have also contributed to local cultural life. Today's residents can hear the Juilliard String Quartet perform on the Library of Congress' Stradivarius violins, blues artist B.B. King perform at the Smithsonian, television journalist David Brinkley discuss his new book at the National Archives, and hundreds more special events offered by these and other agencies every year. Many of these performances are free.

District residents, like tourists, love to visit the Chinese pandas at the National Zoo, fly their kites on the Washington

Monument grounds during the Smithsonian's annual Kite Festival, and become acquainted with the diverse cultures showcased in the Smithsonian's Festival of American Folklife.

Like tourists, they stand in line to join the crowds for the annual Easter Egg Roll on the lawn of the White House or wait eagerly at the Ellipse for the lighting of the National Christmas Tree. During the first week of April, they stroll down to the Tidal Basin to be canopied once again by a giant pink cumulous of cherry blossoms. Then, feeling very much unlike tourists, Washingtonians simply take the subway home.

Chapter Two

ALEXANDRIA AND ARLINGTON COUNTY, VIRGINIA

- -

Urban Partners, Separate Identities

Streets in Old Town Alexandria follow George Washington's neatly drawn grid. Names such as Duke, Royal, and King paid tribute to the Crown. Oronoco Street was named in honor of the oronoco tobacco crop, which was shipped from the wharf at the foot of the street. Photo by Robert Llewellyn

Seen from the long, low approach path along the Potomac, Washington National Airport seems to stand like a link in time between a very old municipality and a very new one. Downriver stand the wharves, warehouses, and restored red-brick downtown of Alexandria, a thriving port city when George Washington and his friends debated issues of freedom there in the years before the Revolution. On the north side of the airport, Arlington County's silver-and-glass corporate towers cluster in a chain of urban centers that were sedate suburban crossroads just a decade ago.

For about 50 years Alexandria and Arlington were a single jurisdiction known as Alexandria, D.C.—cut out of Fairfax County as Virginia's contribution to the original 10-mile-square District of Columbia. About half of Alexandria and all of Arlington still remain within the ruler-straight boundaries of the District plan, which ran in a diagonal northwest from Jones Point (where George Washington set the first District cornerstone) to Falls Church at the western corner, and northeast from Falls Church to the Potomac River at Little Falls. Inside the roughly diamond-shaped site lies some of Northern Virginia's prettiest landscape:

steep, riverfront palisades; sharp, foothill ridges; and deep, hardwood valleys where half a dozen streams cut a rocky course to the Potomac. Fingering commercial areas generously with green space, city and county have retained much of their natural beauty, while growing virtually together— Alexandria to the south, Arlington to the north—into one of the most densely populated corridors in the United States.

Although they have been politically separate from the District since 1847, both city and county have prospered as neighbors to the capital. Alexandria and Arlington today are among the most affluent localities in the nation, both ranking in the top 10 in per capita income. They also rank among the most highly educated communities; more than 40 percent of their adult residents are college graduates.

Most of Northern Virginia's prosperity, as well as most of its settlement, has occurred in the twentieth century, when improved transportation brought its hills and fresh air within commuting distance for the growing federal work force. With the completion of National Airport and Defense Department highways during World War II, the area became a primary gateway through which goods and passengers arrived from the rest of the nation and the world.

Today the stream of commuters and commerce flows both ways. Alexandria and Arlington have emerged from the 1980s as major employment centers for an expanding federal government and for private industry, together adding more than 70,000 jobs to Northern Virginia's economy between 1980 and 1990. With jobs now outnumbering the available work force in both jurisdictions, the area attracts workers from the District as well as from Fairfax and Prince William counties and even suburban Maryland.

These changes have brought the kind of urban amenities such as parks, educational opportunities, and expanded cultural resources that often develop when suburbs mature into cities. They have also brought challenges, as each community learns to meet the needs of populations vastly different from those who lived there just a generation ago and to maintain equilibrium among the

interests of neighborhoods, businesses, developers, commuters, and tourists.

Fortunately, the inheritors of the small swatch of land once known as Alexandria, D.C., are well endowed with the resources (and the will) to manage today's changes and to plan for the future. As the capital region enters its third century, the City of Alexandria and Arlington County are full urban partners whose identities—and destinies—are very much their own.

Alexandria: Past as Prologue

Many people, including most Alexandrians, believed that President George Washington really wanted to make Alexandria the new U.S. capital. In order not to show undue favoritism to his own,

though, he placed the main site of the new federal city on the other side of the river; and, just in case anyone thought he might profit personally from the selection, he decreed that no federal buildings could be built in the territory thereafter known as Alexandria, D.C.

Nevertheless, everyone knew that Washington's heart was in Alexandria. Why else would he place the ceremonial first boundary stone at Jones Point, symbolically joining the capital that would bear his name with the hometown of his youth?

Loyalties aside, George Washington clearly believed that Alexandria would play a role (perhaps the controlling one) in the economic destiny of the region. As

Facing page: Busy National Airport, between Arlington and Alexandria, is a boon to legislators, who cherish its convenience to Capitol Hill. Photo by Rene Sheret/Folio

Above: Metrorail brings National Airport within a few minutes' commute of Arlington's hotels and business centers. Photo by Joseph Sohm/ Chromosohm

Key Bridge spans the Potomac between Rosslyn and Arlington. Early county settlers depended on Mr. Awbrey's ferry for this trip across the river. Photo by Joseph Sohm/Chromosohm

a deep-water seaport, the town would be the District's gateway for oceangoing shipping. It would also be a logical trade center for the produce and raw materials that he expected would soon begin flowing by canal along the Potomac to and from the rich Ohio Valley territories to the west.

Washington certainly had every reason to expect the town to remain a prosperous and cosmopolitan city, as it had been for decades before the Federal District was created.

As early as 1732 Scottish merchants had established a settlement known as Belle Haven at the mouth of Great Hunting Creek. Nearby was the warehouse built by the colony of Virginia where tobacco was inspected and shipped down to the Potomac to other American colonies, Europe, and the Caribbean. Tobacco trade prospered, and the settlement grew. In 1749 a town was incorporated and laid out on 60 acres of riverfront property, most of which was owned by John Alexander. Alexander agreed to sell the property only on the condition that the town would bear his name. Seventeen-year-old George Washington, who lived nine miles downriver with his brother at Mt. Vernon, was hired to help survey the neat grid of 84 half-acre lots along seven streets that overlooked the wharves.

The port had thrived in Colonial days, even when the tobacco crop failed. Mills, bakeries, and breweries for the new wheat-based economy took over the waterfront, and demand for the products was high. Later, international

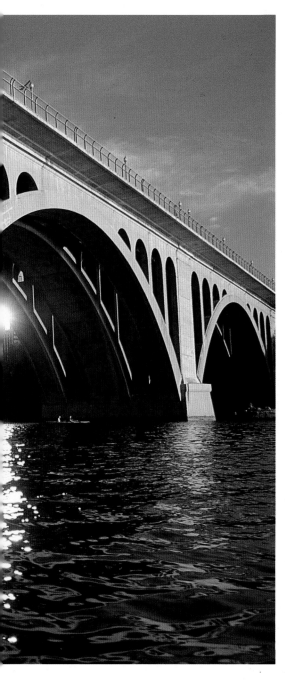

trade continued to improve, and Alexandria merchants looked forward to a new era of prosperity.

That prosperity seemed assured when President Washington included the town of Alexandria and about 30 square miles of surrounding Fairfax County in the site he finally selected for the new Federal District. For a time the new capital did, in fact, depend on Alexandria and its neighboring port of Georgetown for food and other goods. As a catalyst for national or international commerce, however, the city of Washington grew much too slowly to be of any real economic benefit to its neighbors. Stricken by fires, a cholera epidemic, declining shipping trade, and increased competition from railroads, Alexandria saw its economy come almost to a standstill in the 1820s and

trade, which had naturally declined during the Revolutionary War, picked up as soldiers returned to their farms and the high seas became safe once again for shipping.

Believing that he was retired from public service, George Washington began working seriously on plans for a canal that would skirt the great falls of the Potomac north of town. The ensuing venture into interstate commerce illustrated the need to create a federal framework for the highly independent states, a realization that led to the Constitutional Convention shortly thereafter. When Washington became the first President of the new United States government, he abandoned his retirement but not his dreams of a canal. With things thus settled at home and abroad,

1830s. The town's relationship with the federal city was increasingly strained after Washington abolished slave trading and Alexandria did not. Soon dealings broke off entirely as the two sections of the Federal District disagreed over debts for a costly project that linked Alexandria by viaduct with Georgetown and the C & O Canal. In 1846 Congress voted to return Alexandria, D.C., to Virginia.

During the Civil War the U.S. government regarded Alexandria as hostile territory. On May 24, 1861, the opening shots were fired on South Carolina's Fort Sumter, and on May 25 the

New settlers from Central America, Africa, the Caribbean, and Asia renew the cosmopolitan vitality of Alexandria's days as a Colonial seaport. Photo by Joseph Sohm/Chromosohm

Thousands of freed slaves settled in Alexandria communities following the Civil War. Many found work in waterfront oystering and fishing industries. Courtesy, National Archives

New York Zouaves marched across Long Bridge from the capital to occupy Alexandria and the surrounding hills. While the area was under Union protection, thousands of former slaves sought refuge there, joining hundreds of freedmen and women who had settled in Alexandria decades earlier as the plantation economy had declined

In the years following Reconstruction, Alexandria became a quiet southern town with few pretentions to international commerce. Railroad yards replaced the canal, factories and mills took over the waterfront, and the gentry moved up onto the scenic ridges overlooking the town from the north. There they built gracious homes with big front porches in subdivisions they named Rosemont, Braddock Heights, Jefferson Park, and Beverly Hills. Alexandria became, in the words of one Washington belle, "our aristocratic little sister across the river"; and so it remained until the population boom of the 1930s.

Thousands of New Deal and World War II-era federal workers with jobs in the District and at defense installations in Northern Virginia transformed the old city into a large commuter suburb, sending the population skyrocketing from 33,000 in 1940 to 61,000 in 1950. In the postwar decades the city continued to grow in size, filling suburban corridors

with garden, high-rise, and townhouse apartment communities that were convenient to the Pentagon and the growing number of other defense-related offices located in the area.

A regional shopping mall at Landmark, adjacent to Shirley Highway, anchored a new metropolis of commercial and residential towers in the 1960s and 1970s, while old neighborhoods everywhere strained at their boundaries and the city became the most densely populated jurisdiction in the metropolitan area.

Except for the great increase in population, however, Alexandria in the early 1970s was not that much different from the Alexandria of a hundred years earlier. Commercially, it was still a sleepy Southern town with some shops and warehouses but little else in the way of business or industry. Residents were family oriented and predominately middle class; racially, the population was about 14 percent black and almost all the rest white. Practically everyone had been born in the United States.

Alexandria today is a strikingly different place. Mirroring the economic growth throughout the region, the aristocratic little city across the river has become a busy business center, whose concentration of office space is second only to that of Arlington. More than 14

Although George Washington owned a pew at Christ Church, shown here, slippery weather made it necessary to hold his funeral service at the easier-to-reach Old Presbyterian Meeting House. Photo by David Patterson/Carol Highsmith Photography

million square feet of offices now stand in Alexandria's 15.75 square miles; almost 75 percent of that space was constructed during the 1980s. A vast new office corridor is emerging in the once-blighted industrial areas near Metro stations adjacent to I-95, just west of the original Old Town. Corporate centers continue to grow near Shirley Highway at Landmark and Mark Center. New red-brick office complexes blend with Colonial and Victorian-era houses and stores along the Old Town streets that George Washington helped to survey.

During the 1980s employment in Alexandria jumped from 53,000 to more than 84,000 jobs. Many major private em-

ployers are defense related, such as the Institute for Defense Analyses, or defense contractors with a multitude of high-tech products and services. Because of its convenience to the capital, Alexandria has also become a popular location for national associations such as the American Trucking Association and the Boat Owners' Association of the U.S.

The city's cosmopolitan character is reflected in its changing demographics. In recent years Alexandria's abundant employment opportunities and vast supply of reasonably priced rental housing have attracted immigrants from virtually everywhere in the world. Now at least one in seven of the city's

Most Alexandria structures were built with the distinctive red clay bricks produced by factories along the Potomac riverfront. Brickmaking was one of the first local industries. Photo by Joseph Sohm/ Chromosohm

Alexandria's City Hall, built in 1873, has been imaginatively preserved and updated to accommodate the business of the contemporary city. City Hall wraps around Market Square, where local militiamen drilled under orders from George Washington. Photo by Nina Tisara

current residents was born outside of the United States. The city's black population continues to be an important part of the community, in 1990 comprising about 22 percent of the 111,200 people who presently call Alexandria home. About 10 percent of the city's residents are Hispanic, and more than 4 percent are Asian. Modern Alexandria, in fact, looks and feels very much like the international crossroads George Washington envisioned.

It is also filled with many buildings he would probably recognize. His church, a favorite tavern, and some of the first homes built on town lots still stand right where Washington left them. At least a dozen public and private organizations work in various ways to protect the historic structures and many other aspects

of the city's heritage. This happens because an impressive number of Alexandria's citizens have always realized that prosperity was only part of George Washington's legacy. The real gift was, and is, a deeply embedded sense of history and Alexandria's unique place in it.

Old Town, now a national historic district, is one of the nation's foremost cultural and architectural resources. It is also a vibrant urban core for the contemporary city. Within the one-square-mile area, more than 1,000 Colonial, Federal, and Victorian structures have received historic designation and are in public and private use. Many have been restored to museum-quality condition; others have been adapted to contemporary needs, such as the city hall and the 1724 home of John Ramsay, which is now Alexandria's official visitors center. The City's Historic Alexandria office also maintains a museum of local history in the Lyceum, a stately, white Greek Revival school building constructed in 1844 that the City purchased by eminent domain in 1970 to save from being razed. The City also runs a museum at Mr. Gadsby's City Tavern, where George Washington danced with Martha at his annual Birthnight balls. Genealogists treasure the historic books and publications held by Lloyd House Library (part of the public library system), which operates in an elegant townhouse built by a prominent nineteenth-century merchant.

Private, non-profit organizations own the 1850 Athenaeum art and history museum; Robert E. Lee's boyhood home, built in 1795; and the 1795 Lee-Fendall House, which was home to two of Alexandria's most prominent families. Christ Church, where, as the town's most prominent citizen, Washington paid the highest price for the best pew, still holds regular services. The Old Presbyterian Meeting House conducts tours of the sanctuary where Lighthorse Harry Lee delivered Washington's funeral oration, calling him "first in war, first in peace and first in the hearts of his countrymen."

Old Town today offers clear proof that historic preservation efforts have also been a wise investment in the city's future. Its cobbled sidewalks are busy from morning to midnight with shoppers browsing at the window displays of specialty stores, art galleries, and boutiques. Almost 1.5 million tourists visit the city annually, and practically all come to Old Town to see a museum or

two, to join a walking tour led by a Colonial-costumed guide, or to take a narrated tram ride through the town. Business diners and local residents fill the tables of more than 250 restaurants representing most of the world's cuisines.

Such historic districts in other cities often seem like glorified theme parks. Old Town, though, is very much a living community and one of the premiere addresses for business in the Potomac region. Almost half of Alexandria's new office space has been built in or adjacent to Old Town with strict architectural controls insuring that new buildings blend in neatly with old. Townhouses in nearby residential neighborhoods often command prices of $500,000 and more.

A walk along the riverfront shows how deftly redevelopment in Alexandria has been made to serve past, present, and future. Encumbered with decaying factories, warehouses, and other eyesores a little more than a decade ago, the old wharf district began its comeback in 1983, when a World War I naval

High-rise offices, residential condos, and hotels are an urban village in Alexandria's hills. Nearby I-95 brings it close to everything. Photo by Carol Highsmith Photography

weaponry factory was renovated and converted to studio space for more than 150 painters, sculptors, and other artists. Today the Torpedo Factory is Alexandria's top tourist attraction, with more than 800,000 visitors in 1990. The adjacent festival marketplace, restaurant, and offices echo the busy commercial life of Colonial days, when Scottish merchants and craftsmen established shops near the wharves.

At the south end of the waterfront, a recent townhouse development stands on the site of a former Ford manufacturing plant; buried underneath are docks and pilings dating from Colonial days. As the building site was excavated for the new townhouses, urban archaeologists were able to make detailed drawings and photographs of the artifacts and glean important information about the seagoing era. These and other records of the city's early life are preserved at the city's Museum of Archaeology at the Torpedo Factory. Farther north along the waterfront a tidal lock from the canal that once linked Alexandria with Georgetown is on view outside the city's Waterfront Museum. A bike and jogging path follows the waterfront, connecting more than a dozen parks and public places from Jones Point north to Daingerfield Island bordering National Airport.

Respect for their cultural heritage has enabled residential neighborhoods else-

where in the city to maintain their quality of life along with the historic architecture. The Parker-Gray Historic District protects a community known as Uptown, which was established by free blacks as early as 1810. Parker-Gray is also home to Alexandria's Black Resources Center. Several homes and other buildings significant to the city's Afro-American history have been preserved in the community once known as "The Bottoms" and later called "The Dip," which was founded by free blacks as early as 1790.

Several important sites have been preserved as recreational or historic parks, including Fort Ward, one of the major Union defensive posts in the hills northwest of Old Town. A recently discovered gravestone from a nineteenth-century Afro-American cemetery is the focus of a new Black Heritage Park, a nine-acre recreational and historic area in south Alexandria, which has been donated by the developer of the nearby Carlyle office and residential community. In Old Town the Northern Virginia Regional Park Authority maintains the grand mansion built by John Carlyle where British General Edward Braddock stayed in 1755 before leading his troops off to the French and Indian War.

Thanks to a 1989 city ordinance, building sites in historically significant areas now are all studied by professional archaeologists prior to development or rebuilding. As a result, new discoveries are being made about Alexandria's history virtually everywhere in the city. Future development near the I-95 corridor at Landmark and the new Metro station in the Van Dorn area will likely reveal

Stores and houses in Old Town include a variety of styles: Georgian, Federal, Victorian, even Art Moderne. Most cobblestone sidewalks are recent additions. Photo by Nick Sebastian/Photri

more about the commercial grist mills and turnpikes that flourished in those same hills and valley during the nineteenth century. New apartment projects in the high-rise corridor along Duke Street may offer souvenirs of the Union Army's clever attempts to launch hot-air balloons from the high ground there in order to spy on rebel troops encamped farther south during the Civil War.

Excavations for new corporate centers in the important redevelopment zone between the King Street and Eisenhower Metro station may reveal more about Spring Garden, a park and tavern where Washington and his friends cele-

Below: In good weather, folk dancers and singers, representing the many nationalities of county residents, perform in public spaces. Here Polish dancers enliven Alexandria's Market Square. Photo by Nina Tisara

Facing page, bottom: Today's office, retail, and residential developments blend gracefully with renovated historic waterfront structures. Archaeologists documented remnants of Colonial wharves beneath a new townhouse complex. Photo by Roger Foley/Folio

brated the anniversary of the Declaration of Independence in 1798. A planned large-scale residential development on 320 acres formerly used by the Potomac Railroad Yards at the city's north border will give archaeologists the opportunity to look for the foundation of John Alexander's home, built in 1735, and for more remnants of the Alexandria Canal.

In 1991 the city adopted a new master plan that will encourage moderation in future commercial development and provide for additional residential areas. Integral to the plan is a chapter on Alexandria's history describing what happened in each planning area and detailing strategies for preserving its notable resources.

This means that as a matter of policy

as well as of fact, the builders of Alexandria's future will continue to acknowledge the contributions bequeathed by their fellow citizens for more than 250 years. And with every bit of progress they create, they will contribute something of their own to that legacy.

Arlington County: The Way Home

At the close of the Civil War, Northern Virginians found little still standing of the world they remembered. Four years of occupation by a hostile Union Army had effectively wiped out the local economy, shutting down businesses and driving many citizens from their homes.

Outside Alexandria's town limits, the hilly countryside that would become Arlington County fared worst of all. Small farms, repeatedly stripped of crops and livestock to feed hungry troops, lay abandoned by their frustrated owners. Great tracts of hardwood forests had been razed to give defending soldiers better sightlines and to deny invaders any place to hide. Government and services were virtually nonexistent.

On a ridge above the Potomac, Robert E. Lee's Arlington House, once a link with the Colonial plantation era, now stood as a symbol of a hopeful but much different future. Two hundred acres of lawns directly in front of the mansion's neoclassical, white portico had become a National Cemetery, the resting place for thousands of Union War dead. On other portions of the Arlington grounds, Federal troops remained at Fort Whipple, which was later renamed Fort Myer; and thousands of former slaves were building new lives in Freedmen's Village, a resettlement camp provided by the U.S. government

Separated from the city of Alexandria when Virginia was readmitted to the Union in 1870, Arlington County was built—or rebuilt—literally from the ground up during the next few decades. Walls of new schools and stores were made of sturdy bricks formed of Arlington's abundant red riverfront clay, which also became the basis of the county's

Left: A chain of parks and pathways curves along Alexandria's waterfront. Historic markers observe that ocean-going vessels once sailed into this Potomac River bay. Photo by Joseph Sohm/Chromosohm

industrial economy. By the turn of the century, Arlington produced more bricks than any other place in the nation. Towns such as Glencarlyn and Barcroft grew from settlements established at prewar railway stations, and new subdivisions at Ballston and Cherrydale were built along electric trolley lines that had supplanted railroad tracks at the turn of the century. Rural, and pretty much on their own politically, the communities built strong local governments based on active volunteer participation. Good Citizens Leagues prospered in the same spirit as church socials and volunteer fire departments.

The Good Citizens movement came into its own at the turn of the century when reformers took aim at the general lawlessness that reigned in rough saloon districts along the Potomac waterfront. In Rosslyn farmers were routinely ambushed and robbed as they returned from produce markets across the bridge in Georgetown; the bodies of many were dropped into a gulch cynically nicknamed "Dead Man's Hollow." At the border with Alexandria, ne'er-do-wells congregated at St. Asaph's horse racing and gambling house and several lesser dens of iniquity nearby. By 1904 the good citizens of Arlington had had enough. In a midnight raid led by zealous Commonwealth Attorney Crandal Mackey, an axe-wielding posse smashed up the race track and established a tradition of citizen activism that remains just as strong in Arlington today.

That tradition has come to be known as "The Arlington Way." Through the years it has grown into a sensitive infrastructure of citizen participation at every level of community activity: neighborhood associations, interest groups, task forces, and advisory commissions to the county board. The system is informal and the definition varies, but the

Above: John Carlyle, one of several Scottish merchants and traders who originally settled the city, built this mansion on a bluff overlooking the wharves so he could keep an eye on his ships. Photo by Joseph Sohm/Chromosohm

Left: Despite its growth, Alexandria remains true to its tradition of civic involvement. It boasts Northern Virginia's only full-time professional resident theater company and a number of strong community arts groups. Photo by Larry Ghiorsi/Brooklyn Image Group

Old soldiers return to Arlington Cemetery to participate in solemn ceremonies or to stroll quiet pathways. More than 200,000 graves stand upon the 612 acres. Photo by Joseph Sohm/Chromosohm

process is effective. When an issue arises, citizens speak out, listen to each other, form coalitions and alliances, and, more often that not, find a solution with which most people can live.

Such grass-roots participation might be difficult to maintain in some of the sprawling neighboring counties elsewhere in the region, but Arlington's 26-square-mile area is compact enough that its 170,000 residents can think of each other as neighbors. All of the county is a single jurisdiction with no incorporated towns within its limits, and all members of the county board are elected at large. This means that each board member represents the whole county and every resident.

During the 1930s and 1940s, Arlington struggled to maintain its cohesive, small-town character as the New Deal and World War II brought thousands of federal workers into the area. Many of the newcomers were allied with the Pentagon, the Navy Annex, and other defense installations whose massive presence dominated the southern portion of the county, cutting through it with highways and unaccustomed traffic. As the population jumped from 26,615 in 1930 to 135,449 in 1950, giant apartment complexes, including Colonial Village and Buckingham, were hastily built along the riverfront, and tidy neighborhoods of red-brick homes were laid out in hilly suburban reaches. The new neighborhoods formed civic associations of their own; citizens

groups sponsored projects to back the war effort; and federal and defense workers joined community groups such as the War Production Board Symphony Orchestra. In time they all became part of the Arlington Way.

Citizen activism reached a new level of effectiveness during the 1970s, when neighborhood associations and other groups closed ranks to challenge the proposed routing of I-66. Arlingtonians protested that the expressway, which is the only interstate road that feeds directly into Washington, D.C., would funnel thousands of rush-hour commuters through residential neighborhoods. They feared that noise and air pollution, high-density development, and other changes that accompany interstate highways would change the character of the county forever, and that the giant gash created by an eight-lane roadbed would effectively sever Arlington's much-prized cohesion. Homeowners formed a committee, the Arlington Coalition on Transportation, which fought the project politically and in the courts for 10 years. Finally citizens, local government, and the Department of Transportation achieved a compromise that allowed a road four-lanes wide to be built, along with buffers, parks, and other concessions that would keep the impact on the community to a minimum.

During the 1960s and 1970s, citizens also worked with the county board and the Washington Metropolitan Area Mass Transit Authority to determine the route that the coming Metrorail system would take through the county. After considerable discussion, a consensus was reached to run the line along Wilson Boulevard, one of the county's oldest commercial thoroughfares, and to redevelop the areas surrounding most of the 11 Metrorail stations into new urban centers.

Partially because of those earlier decisions, Arlington is being challenged again. This time the county is confronting sweeping and fundamental changes that social scientists call the urbanization of Arlington County.

During the past decade the population has risen only slightly, but everything else about Arlington County has begun to look and feel very much like a contemporary city. As Metrorail and I-66

brought Arlington's reasonably priced land within minutes of the capital, federal agencies and private corporations hurried to relocate in the county. In just 10 years 41,000 new jobs were created, transforming Arlington from a bedroom suburb into a major employment center that now draws commuters from western counties and even from Washington, D.C. To accommodate them, postmodern glass, brick, and steel office towers have risen in urban groupings through-

out the county, doubling the available office space during the 1980s from 14 million to 28 million square feet. Almost three-quarters of that new space—10 million square feet—was built between 1985 and 1990.

Drawn by business and encouraged by continuing improvements to National Airport (a brief Metro ride away at the county's southern border), record numbers of travelers began to regard Arlington as a destination of choice, spending

Lively postmodern office and residential architecture brings a little contrast and a lot of drama to Arlington's historic Courthouse district. Photo by Larry Ghiorsi/Brooklyn Image Group

Elevated skywalks and lively, underground shopping arcades make it easy to get from high-rise to high-rise in Crystal City. Photo by Greg Pease

a record one billion dollars there in 1989. Several new hotels, including luxury chains such as Grand Hyatt and Ritz Carlton, were built to serve this growing demand. In 1991 travelers could choose from 34 hotels with more than 9,000 rooms in business and pleasure travel destinations throughout the county.

Thanks to comprehensive land-use plans drawn up with considerable citizen collaboration during the 1960s, most of the area's commercial growth has taken place in those well-defined urban centers surrounding Metrorail stations. The plan thus concentrates high-density development westward from Rosslyn to Ballston in the center of the county and south along the waterfront from Rosslyn to Crystal City.

More than half of the new construction has risen at the Ballston station, which is becoming the county's "downtown" of the 1990s. The area has been familiar to travelers since the early nineteenth century when one of the first settlers ran a tavern called Ball's Ordinary; and, later, a rural community grew here at the intersection of two well-traveled highways. Modern Ballston intersects Metrorail and I-66, which makes it an easy-to-reach destination from almost anywhere in the capital region. The growing community includes new condos, a 250-room hotel, and a dramatic atrium shopping mall as well as offices for a growing roster of organizations, including the Department of the Interior's Fish and Wildlife Service, the Department of Immigration and Naturalization, the Hecht Company, and the United States Life Insurance Company (USLICO).

Ballston is presently the site of George Mason University's International Institute, which includes the Center for European Community Studies. The first such facility in the United States, the CECS offers graduate courses and other programs studying the new single-Europe market as well as the nation's only EC Documentation Center, where students and business can access all reports, periodicals, and other information produced by the European community.

Farther along the Ballston-Rosslyn Corridor, Virginia Square is slated to emerge as the county's intellectual and cultural center. The area is presently home to the law school and Metro campus of George Mason University, the central Arlington Public Library, and a campus and training center for the Federal Deposit Insurance Corporation.

With its town square of family-run businesses, original streamline moderne offices and stores, and its grassy War Memorial Park in the middle of Wilson Boulevard, Arlington's oldest commercial district in Clarendon has begun to reemerge as a low-rise "urban village." In contrast, at Courthouse Station the hills surrounding Arlington County's 1896 red-brick courthouse have become popular sites for dramatically styled concrete-and-glass high-rise offices and condos, including expansive new facilities for the county government.

With their dramatic views of the Potomac and easy access to Washington, D.C., Rosslyn and Crystal City were Arlington's earliest urban centers. Together they now provide more than 19 million square feet of office space, including the twin silver skyscrapers owned by the Gannett Corporation and its national newspaper, *USA Today*, which frame Rosslyn's steep riverfront hills.

More than 100,000 people now work in the Rosslyn-Crystal City corridor, which adjoins the Pentagon and National Airport to the south. Most are employed in aerospace and defense-related industries or at one of several federal agencies headquartered in the area. Rising between these older centers, Pentagon City is fast becoming a favored location for corporate offices, including the Mid-Atlantic headquarters of giant MCI Communications. With a striking design reminiscent of a Victorian garden conservatory, Fashion Centre at Pentagon City attracts shoppers from throughout the region to upscale stores such as Nordstrom and Macy's. The mixed-use development also includes offices, condos, and a 17-story Ritz Carlton Hotel.

As Arlington has grown to look like a

Above: Playful, modern sculpture enhances the exterior of this Rosslyn high-rise. More than 100,000 people now work in the Rosslyn-Crystal City corridor. Photo by Jack Novak/Photri

Facing page: All that glitters is on sale somewhere in the expansive new Fashion Centre in Pentagon City. A regional mall virtually in the city, the complex also boasts a luxury hotel. Photo by Carol Highsmith Photography

city, the people who live there now bear a striking resemblance to city dwellers: they are younger, better educated, more culturally and racially diverse, and less likely to be married than the suburban Arlingtonians of a generation ago. Those who are married have fewer children or none at all; the average household size in Arlington County is now fewer than two. Almost two-thirds of the county's residents live in rental housing.

This dramatic demographic shift is another of the changes masked by the county's deceptively stable population figure. In reality, as Arlington families have moved westward into the big backyards of Fairfax County, young singles moved into Arlington at nearly an equal rate to take advantage of the new employment opportunities there as well as the relatively lower cost of housing nearby.

While many of the newcomers migrated over from the District or from other regions of the U.S., in recent years fully one-quarter of all people who have moved into Arlington County were born outside the United States.

Arlington's first great wave of foreign-born in-migrants arrived in the 1970s from postwar Vietnam. More than 20,000 Vietnamese settled in the county, and many opened restaurants and shops in the commercial district of Clarendon, which quickly claimed the nickname "Little Saigon." During the 1980s new arrivals from Central America have also established communities in Arlington, along with individuals and families from virtually every country in the world. By 1991 at least one in seven Arlingtonians was born outside the U.S. with more than 50 primary languages, including Korean, Portuguese, Urdu, and Swahili, spoken by Arlington's public schoolchildren.

Of course, Arlingtonians have also experienced the sweeping changes in family life that the 1970s and 1980s have brought to communities throughout the United States. Here, too, most mothers have full-time jobs outside the home, and of the households with children, many are headed by a single parent.

Such dramatic changes can and do transform other communities forever. Arlington, though, still looks and feels a

Food critics say that the finest Vietnamese cuisine outside of Ho Chi Minh City can be found in Arlington's charming art deco Clarendon district. Neighborhood gourmets agree. Photo by Joseph Sohm/ Chromosohm

Some things never change. Arlingtonians enjoy finding fresh regional produce at weekly farmers markets, a longtime county tradition. Photo by Nina Tisara

lot like it always has, with its red-brick neighborhoods still intact and its citizens active as always. In fact, Arlington has embraced its growing diversity as a source of new people and resources that can be allied in a multitude of ways to make the community more cohesive and stronger than ever.

At the heart of Arlington—and the Arlington Way—are the neighborhood civic associations that keep residents active in community projects, work with the county board and others to protect neighborhood interests, and even sponsor block parties and other sociable events. Formed in 1914, the Federation of Civic Associations is an umbrella organization for the local groups and has long been recognized as a formidable champion of the county's hometown character and human scale.

On any given issue dozens of other groups may make their voices heard. Among these are standing organizations such as the Arlington Heritage Alliance, which works to preserve historic sites, ad hoc commissions, advisory panels, and task forces formed by the county board and others.

In recent years public-private partnerships—county-sponsored alliances of developers, local businesses, nearby civic associations, and other community organizations—have proved an effective way to bring the Arlington Way into new high-density urban centers.

In Clarendon, the Clarendon Alliance works with developers to relocate small businesses displaced by urban renewal, to preserve some of the area's excellent art deco and streamline moderne commercial buildings, and to promote the family-owned Vietnamese and Latino restaurants that are among the best in the capital region.

The Ballston Partnership would like residents of nearby neighborhoods to stroll over to the new downtown for Saturday shopping, Sunday brunch, or a pleasant evening's walk. To encourage such pleasantries, the Partnership has developed a lively "Festival Street," with banners, plantings, local fairs, and a Saturday Flower Mart. Members also actively promote the use of Metro's Transit Store, which makes it easy for thousands of people employed in Ballston to take advantage of public transportation.

Older urban centers also benefit from the partnership approach. In Rosslyn, where "first generation" high-rise and mid-rise office buildings are being remodeled, the Rosslyn Renaissance will help realign parks, skywalks, and retail areas into a more cohesive urban neighborhood. Outside of the high-density corridor, the Columbia Pike Revitalization Organization beautifies and promotes a community of small businesses in a postwar-era commercial neighborhood that serves a nearby Latino community.

The partnership approach has inspired informal cooperative projects among various interests in many areas of community life. At Ballston the developer of the new Ellipse building offered to donate space for a visual arts gallery; the county agreed to run it, and the community gained a popular amenity. Crystal City developer Charles E. Smith built and donated the spectacular Water Park, where a broad waterfall is the backdrop for an outdoor stage that the county's cultural affairs division fills with free performances by local musicians and dancers as well as folk artists from the local immigrant communities.

The Workplace Literacy Project is a good example of just how innovative and mutually beneficial such cooperative ventures can be. Funded by federal and state grants, Arlington's public schools and the local hotel industry designed a program to teach English-language and community-living skills on the job to the hundreds of recent immigrants on the hotels' work forces. The project helps the hotels recruit, train, and maintain good employees and helps the workers adjust more readily to their new community.

As newcomers settle into Arlington's historic neighborhoods and new office towers just blocks from wilderness parks, government and citizens also find mutual reward in encouraging the local traditions that bridge Arlington County's past, present, and future. Community arts groups, such as the Arlington Symphony, which began as the War Production Board Orchestra in 1946, receive free rehearsal and performance space in recycled school and community buildings provided by the county. Visual artists receive studio and exhibition space. Several of the buildings given or leased at low cost to community organizations have historic value, such as the 1910 Maury School, which is the home of the Arlington Arts Center at Virginia Square, or the Hume School building which is the home of the Arlington Historical Society. And thanks to the persistence of the County Extension Service, Arlingtonians can still find the freshest cucumbers and tomatoes each Saturday at Farmer's Market, relocated to a nearby parking lot, after a new jail took over

on the market's traditional stand on Courthouse Square.

Through the Arlington Housing Corporation and other projects, Arlingtonians also work to preserve neighborhoods by keeping attractive, affordable housing in the county. The Corporation encourages partnerships among government and public agencies, citizens, and developers so that desirable properties such as older garden apartment com-

plexes can be acquired and maintained for low- and moderate-income families. To make sure that the 1935 Colonial Village, home to Arlington's first wave of new government workers, would remain affordable to current residents, Arlington groups had portions of the project protected as a historic landmark, which is managed by AHC. In commercial neighborhoods the county-run Business Conservation Program helps small businesses remain competitive in older neighborhoods by assisting in the design of new storefronts, signs, and other exterior improvements.

In an era when progress is usually accompanied by a bulldozer, change is rarely so subtle here or anywhere else in the Potomac region. Citizens of Arlington tend to be a little more confident about the future though, knowing that they have participated actively in its planning.

In a way they are still building their community brick by brick. That would, of course, be the Arlington Way.

Thanks to alliances of preservationists and the business community, prewar multifamily housing, such as Colonial Village, is now home to communities of young families. Photo by Jake McGuire/ Washington Stock Photo

Chapter Three

MONTGOMERY COUNTY, MARYLAND

. . . .

Making the Good Life Better

J ust as the classical cityscape of Washington, D.C., symbolizes the ideals of democracy in the New World, Montgomery County looks a lot like the American Dream.

In many ways it is suburbia idealized, with pretty, close-knit communities, a responsive government, and an active cultural and spiritual life. Children can study in a public school system that consistently produces the highest average Scholastic Aptitude Test scores in the region, or they can attend one of the 202 private schools in the county. On weekends they play Little League baseball, soccer, or tennis on hundreds of well-run public facilities or exercise their ponies at one of three equestrian centers.

Their parents might join a local polo league or play golf at one of more than two dozen courses in the county, including some of the nation's most famous private clubs. They shop for designer necessities at any of four regional malls, nosh on bagels and lox in a downtown neighborhood deli, and hear a string quartet perform Mozart in the paneled music room of a Georgian mansion. They can even spend low-budget afternoons climbing the rugged scenic trails of Sugarloaf Mountain at Montgomery's rural western border or paddling a canoe along one of the dozens of unspoiled creeks and rivers that run down

Gracious Victorian homes in communities throughout Montgomery County provide a hometown core for today's growing suburbs. Photo by Carol Highsmith Photography

Right: Montgomery County was named for General Richard Montgomery (1738-1775), who fought in the Revolutionary War. Painting by Charles Willson Peale. Courtesy, Independence National Historic Park. From Cirker, *Dictionary of American Portraits*

Below: The U.S. Army Corps of Engineers constructed Montgomery County's Cabin John Bridge to carry both traffic and the main water supply conduit for the District of Columbia. The men in the foreground were building a 220-foot-long stone arch support for the bridge. From the Robert G. Merrick Archive, Maryland State Archives

through the county toward the Chesapeake.

In the grand tradition of American dreams, the good life in Montgomery County more often than not comes as the reward for enterprise and hard work. Residents here are high achievers—an astonishing 35 percent of all adults have attended graduate school or earned an advanced degree. Of an overall population of 751,000, more than 450,000 are in the work force, including about two-thirds of the adult women.

It is not surprising, then, that the median household income in Montgomery County ranks first among all counties in Maryland and 14th in the United States; or that household income has grown faster here than anywhere else in the region. Almost 20,000 entrepreneurs—including 6,200

blacks, Asians, and Hispanics classified as "minorities"—own or run local businesses. These enterprises encompass everything from small biotechnical R & D labs, family farms, and Chinese restaurants to the giant Marriott Corporation, whose hotel and food-service operations circle the world. Prominent citizens whose mansions oversee the Potomac along River Road are among the metropolitan area's most noteworthy doers: business leaders, top doctors and lawyers, Cabinet secretaries, and senior bureaucrats.

That work ethic comes naturally to Montgomery County. Stretching westward for almost 30 miles above the Potomac River fall line, Montgomery County's fertile uplands were settled by yeoman farmers decades after gentleman pioneers had carved the more accessible Tidewater counties into giant plantations. Many of

the county's first citizens came from other colonies that already had grown too crowded for them. There were Germans from Pennsylvania, Quakers from eastern Maryland, and second sons from southern Virginia estates. Others were indentured servants, many of them Scottish, who had worked off their servitude and sought a new start. Although a few assembled large land holdings here, most of the settlers held small patents of about 200 acres, which many worked without slaves.

Like their more affluent neighbors to the east, Montgomery County farmers raised tobacco, rolling the crop along old Indian trails down to a natural harbor just below the final set of Potomac rapids at the county's eastern edge. In 1747 an inspection station was established at the port to guarantee the quality of the product; as at Alexandria, Virginia, eight miles downriver, a settlement of merchants, craftsmen, and traders quickly grew around the warehouse. In 1751 a town named Georgetown was surveyed and incorporated.

Another settlement grew around Hungerford's Tavern, which stood at a crossroads on the main road west from Georgetown. In June 1774 local leaders stood at one of the tavern's rough wooden tables to sign their names to a document supporting the people of Boston, who were enduring the Crown's recriminations for their notorious Tea Party. The statement, in part, resolved unanimously, "That it is the opinion of this meeting that the most effectual means of securing of American freedom will be to break off all commerce with Great Britain and the West Indies until the said act be repealed and the right of taxation given up on permanent principles." These "Hungerford Resolves," like the Fairfax Resolves penned in Virginia, set the tone for the Declaration of Independence adopted by the Continental Congress two years later.

The village at Hungerford's became the county seat when Montgomery County, along with neighboring Wash-

ington County to the north, was partitioned out of Frederick County on September 6, 1776, just two months after the Declaration was signed. The southernmost of the new counties was named for General Richard Montgomery of New York, who fell while leading American troops in the Battle of Quebec. Thus Montgomery and Washington were the first counties to be established by the elected representatives of an American sovereign state; they were also the first to be named in honor of Americans rather than European royalty. The county seat was called Montgomery Court House for a while; later it was renamed

Rockville for Rock Creek, which ran through the town.

Revolution and independence affected Montgomery County in personal and domestic ways. Farmers marched to Massachusetts, New York, Pennsylvania, and Virginia with units of the Continental Army and then returned with the peace to restore their neglected farms. The tobacco economy was already suffering the effects of overfarming along with a depressed market worldwide; gradually the crop was replaced by wheat and other grains. When the new District of Columbia incorporated Georgetown along with some 69 square

Montgomery County tobacco farmers spent an entire year working their crop. Spring was for sowing, summer for growing, fall for drying, and winter for stripping the leaves and packing them into hogsheads for shipment to England. Courtesy, Historic St. Mary's City

Above: Conduit lines for Washington's telephone wires were laid along trolley tracks in suburban Maryland about 1910. From the Robert G. Merrick Archive, Maryland State Archives

Right: Maryland commuters in Washington prepare to board an electric streetcar for the trip home to Chevy Chase. By 1903 the trip from the Treasury Department to Chevy Chase took exactly 35 minutes by streetcar. Courtesy, Chevy Chase Historical Society

miles of farmland and streams on the Maryland side, the county lost its only real commercial venue but looked forward to a generous payback down the road.

In reality the road to economic prosperity—and, indeed, most routes of any kind—led westward during the early decades of the nineteenth century. Construction of the C&O Canal, which bypassed the Potomac's falls to open trade with western Maryland, Pennsylvania, and Ohio, was begun in 1828, providing work for local quarrymen and laborers and access to deepwater ports for farmers in the county's western reaches. The

main roads through the county also led west, in the direction of Frederick, the county seat of Washington County and the governmental and commercial center of the region. Except for the trading port of Georgetown, the struggling capital to the east seemed hardly worth the trouble to get there.

Having few roads, no railroads, and little else of strategic value, the county saw only a few skirmishes during the Civil War. It was, however, well armed, as Federal generals took advantage of the county's high ground to emplace several key forts and batteries. One of these posts was on Sugar Loaf Mountain, the highest point in the county, whose 854-foot elevation across the Potomac from the rebel stronghold of Leesburg gave Union Troops a spy's-eye view of Virginia.

Like the Revolution, the Civil War divided county citizens into secessionists and loyalists. This time, though, it was the rebel sympathizers who maintained a low profile, intimidated by the Federal presence just across the District line as well as the thousands of Union soldiers encamped in the county at Poolesville and Darnestown. Most of the 13,000

white residents who had held a total of 5,000 slaves before the war supported the South; but influential Quaker communities centered in Brookeville, Sandy Spring, and other small towns made the county a stronghold of abolitionists as well.

Such disruptions and general unease effectively put an end to most community life and commerce for the duration of the war. Farms were once again neglected or abandoned; and any crops they managed to produce were, more often than not, commandeered by whichever army happened to be passing through. After the war remaining local farmers were joined by immigrants from the north, and together they built a new economy supplying produce to the fast-growing District of Columbia.

In 1873 a cross-county branch of the B & O Railroad finally provided a cheap, fast transportation link with the capital. County workers found it possible to commute to jobs in the city, and Washingtonians found that the breezy highlands of Montgomery County were a refreshing change from swampy capital summers. Many city dwellers chose to resettle in the ample Victorian homes being built in the new commuter suburbs that grew up near stations along the railroad line.

By the turn of the century, expansive hotels and resorts above the Potomac and in other scenic areas were destinations of choice among the fashionable—soon followed by the city's growing middle class. The Chautauqua meeting ground at Glen Echo lured the intelligentsia to an earnest regimen of concerts, lectures, and self-improvement programs. Gilded Age tycoons acquired country estates at the rural end of Wisconsin Avenue to achieve relief from their Dupont Circle mansions. Electric trolleys brought prospective home buyers to enthusiastically advertised new communities in Chevy Chase, Takoma Park, Gaithersburg, Kensington, Garrett Park, and "Peerless Rockville." Garden clubs were formed and volunteer bands played Sunday con-

certs in community bandstands. The good life had indeed arrived in Montgomery County.

Marked only by a line on a map and those barely remembered stone markers, the border between Montgomery County and the District's northwest

suburbs became increasingly hazy. County dairy and vegetable farmers on their way to downtown markets passed through a widening arc of neighborhoods devoted to substantial brick homes, green lawns, and trees, from Rockville almost to Georgetown, from Kensington to Kalorama Heights. With an eye to their mutual interest in maintaining a clean water supply, the neighboring jurisdictions formed the Washington Suburban Sanitary Commission; other such regional organizations soon followed.

As the federal work force expanded between the wars, Montgomery County's well-groomed communities attracted many of the high-level professionals moving into the capital region for a stint of public service. In keeping with Maryland's founding tenet of religious toleration, the area became home to a thriving Jewish community, which found relief here from discriminatory housing and social practices found in other jurisdictions. Apartment buildings became familiar sights; and commercial centers in

A rustic grocery store stands amid the snowy, rural Montgomery County landscape in 1940. Photo by Arthur Rothstein, Farm Security Administration. Courtesy, Library of Congress

Above: The 1907 Poolesville National Bank Building was converted into a town hall. Poolesville, in Montgomery County's westernmost reaches, remains a relatively rural area. Photo by Dave Kelsey

Bethesda and Silver Spring brought urban conveniences uptown.

Mindful that clean air benefits both body and spirit, the government found Montgomery County the ideal site for research laboratories and medical facilities, including the David W. Taylor Naval Research and Development Center, the National Naval Medical Center, the Army Map Service, and, in 1953, the Clinical Center of the National Institutes of Health. By the time the Capital Beltway opened in 1964, more than 350,000 people called Montgomery County home. Most of those homes were "inside the beltway," within a few miles of the District border.

Recent years have changed the appearance, if not the spirit, of Montgomery County as the population edges outward to more affordable land and housing in the county's northern and western reaches. Like other locations bordering the District, Montgomery County's close-in communities have become high-powered, high-density urban centers, packed with new office buildings, condos, restaurants, and stores. The population of these new downtowns has also become increasingly urban—older, wealthier, and more diverse. An increasing percentage of the county's residents was born outside of the U.S.; many are immigrants committed to finding their own places in the American Dream.

A drive west or north from the District line is a little like a trip back in time. Just down the road from contemporary cities and suburban sprawl, Victorian town squares and neighborhoods still preside over growing communities. Farther out, rural towns remain the center of commerce and social life for local family farmers—just as they have since Colonial times.

It is easy to enjoy the contrast between past and present in communities such as Laytonsville, Barnesville, and Brookeville, historic towns still relatively insulated by farms and parkland from the effects of development. Laytonsville was a rural crossroads when it was

settled in the mid-nineteenth century; many original farm-style houses still line its peaceful streets. Barnesville, on the Old Baltimore Road just across the border from Frederick County, is one of the county's smallest towns and, quite possibly, its most secluded outpost. Brookeville, founded in 1794, was later home to an influential Quaker community that founded one of the county's first schools, the Brookeville Academy. The town became a footnote in U.S. Presidential history when James Madison, fleeing British invaders in August 1814, spent a night there as the guest of postmaster Caleb Bentley. Bentley's two-story white house is one of several local landmarks.

and forth across the river at the end of a country highway.

Closer in, Washington Grove, bordering the growing city of Gaithersburg, was originally a camp meeting ground chartered in 1874 by the Methodist Church. Later the town hosted Chautauqua-style programs and became a family-oriented summer resort. Vintage trees still shade the Grove's Victorian town center, and it is still favored as a place to raise a family.

Garrett Park was a Victorian commuter suburb whose developer chose to recreate an English village. The town's purposefully quaint streets, gabled architecture, and country gardens have earned the entire town a listing in the National Register of Historic Places. Farther south, Kensington was another turn-of-the-century model community, popular as a summer home for Washington merchants and gentry. Kensington has been surrounded by automobile-inspired suburban development for a long time, but its old town historic district remains a pleasant place to stroll past fine Queen Anne and Georgian Revival homes that hold court along quiet side streets.

Above the Potomac, about two miles west of the District line, Glen Echo is another community with a Victorian core. It remains surrounded by some of the region's prettiest scenery and is close to some of its most exclusive country clubs. American Red Cross founder Clara Barton moved to Glen Echo when it was still a Chautauqua meeting ground. Her home is now a national historic site administered by the U.S. National Park Service. Glen Echo Park, which was a popular riverside amusement park well into the 1960s, is now an "arts park," with studio, performance, and exhibition space for local writers, actors, sculptors, and painters. Children can ride the park's Dentzel carousel, which still oompahs nicely.

Chevy Chase Village, named after an English hunting ground, was designed to

Although the population in and around Poolesville is approaching 10,000, the town in the county's westernmost thrust remains pleasantly rural. A thriving community before the Civil War, its location just down the road from White's Ferry across the Potomac made it an ideal billet for Union troops, who frequently found occasion to chase rebel forays across the river into Virginia. Today Poolesville is the heart of the county's agricultural industry. White's Ferry, now motorized, shuttles commuters and their cars back

bring the amenities of the manorial lifestyle home to American aristocrats. Crowning Connecticut Avenue at the District Line, the "model community" begun in 1890 offered spacious homes, generous lawns, strict architectural controls, a nearby amusement park, and even grounds for fox hunting. Other communities, also bearing some variant of the name Chevy Chase, were developed nearby. Today they all blend into a serene, affluent enclave that also encompasses the adjacent town of Somerset.

Montgomery County surrounds the cities of Rockville and Gaithersburg as well as most of the city of Takoma Park. Rockville, the county seat since 1776, is a city of almost 50,000, whose Victorian historic district contrasts dramatically with the high-tech development at its suburban edges. On the stage line between Georgetown and Frederick, nineteenth-century Rockville was a convenient gathering place for farmers, merchants, and politicians and home to the Montgomery County Fair. After the railroad arrived, it became a resort and then a year-round suburb that was advertised as "Peerless Rockville." As the National Naval Hospital, the National Institutes of Health, and other federal research facilities settled, one by one, on the county's side of Wisconsin Avenue, the Rockville area evolved into a preeminent center of medical and biotechnical research. Recently it has become home to major educational facilities as well.

Montgomery County's 1891 red-brick courthouse shares Rockville's downtown landscape with its block-long Greek Revival replacement, built in the 1930s. Nearby stands a contemporary concrete-and-glass judicial center. Across the plaza is the high-rise home of the county's executive offices. Multicolored banners, underwritten by local businesses, promote *esprit* in public spaces.

In the spring of 1991, a young black bear strolled onto the grounds of the National Institute of Standards and Technology in the heart of Gaithersburg. The bear had mating, not metaphors, on his mind; but he also inspired a few curious commuters to remark on the comfortable way that past and progress have always intertwined in this city of 40,000.

On a trail cut by Seneca Indians and later used as a "rolling road" by local tobacco farmers, Gaithersburg was a settlement as early as 1765, and a hotel

A gracious Victorian riverside resort and suburb, Glen Echo carefully maintains its turn-of-the-century charm. Photo by Carol Highsmith Photography

Above and right: The city's premiere amusement park for 70 years, Glen Echo Park now offers studio and exhibition space to local artists and performers. Top photo by Joseph Sohm/Chromosohm; inset photo by Michael Ventura/Folio

there was a popular waystation for travelers a century later. After the railroad arrived the town became home to some of the area's most prosperous and innovative citizens. Among these was Edwin Smith, who calculated the earth's orbital wobble from the astral observations he made from the Gaithersburg Latitude Observatory, which he designed and operated there in 1900. Another was William H. Wilmont, who perfected the popular Zoysia variety of lawn grass at Summit Hall Turf Farm, where he established the county's still-thriving sod-farming industry.

Modern Gaithersburg's city hall is a landmark Queen Anne mansion creatively adapted to serve as an efficient center for citizens and services. Dozens of other vintage structures, including Edwin Smith's carefully preserved observatory, are nearby. In the center of the city, NIST's wooded campus is home to federal programs that are defining tomorrow's technologies and today serve as a magnet to dozens of private enterprises in communications, artificial intelligence, and many others.

Just outside Gaithersburg are two new towns that represent opposite ends of the modern spectrum of theories on "ideal communities." Montgomery Village, begun in the 1960s, emphasizes high-density cluster development, open green space, and plenty of amenities such as tennis courts and swimming pools. Nearby Kentlands, a new town of the 1990s, is being built around well-remembered small town conventions such as a downtown shopping and business district, old-fashioned city blocks with quiet side streets, and houses whose porches are purposely placed within waving distance of the sidewalks.

Kentlands might well have been inspired by Takoma Park, itself a model community of the Victorian era and now on the National Register of Historic Places. In the highlands edging the District's northeast border and spilling into Prince George's County and the District, the new town was named for an Indian word meaning "near heaven" and at first was promoted as an escape from Washington's summers.

A devout teetotaler and vegetarian, developer Benjamin Franklin Gilbert conceived his community as a natural extension of his clean-living principles, and through the years Takoma Park has continued to be a place where ideals and ordinances often intertwine. In 1904 the town became home to the world headquarters of the Seventh Day Adventist Church, whose views on physical and spiritual health were similar to Gilbert's own. The Church, in turn, gave the county its first hospital, which evolved into the highly regarded Washington Adventist Hospital, and its first college, today called Columbia Union.

In later years Takoma Park has been home to a succession of freethinkers, commune dwellers, and political activists who have declared their community a nuclear-free zone and placed environmental and social causes on the city's agenda. The city is also popular with young parents who find the old-fashioned neighborhoods of Victorian mansions and 1930s bungalows to be good places to raise their families.

Several of the county's largest urban centers are not cities at all, but rather unincorporated places that have grown around busy transportation corridors. Bethesda, where some 80,000 people live in a densely populated wedge between Wisconsin Avenue and River Road, straddles the route of one of the region's oldest Indian footpaths, which, much later, became the main toll road from Georgetown to Frederick. Near the post office downtown, a monument called the *Madonna of the Trail* commemorates the European-American settlers who passed along the road on their way west.

Named for an early nineteenth century Presbyterian meetinghouse, which was, in turn, named for the healing Pool of Bethesda described by St. John in the New Testament, the community of Bethesda was the site of several of the area's first commuter suburbs. It has been growing steadily since the federal government opened the National Naval Medical Center on the road to Rockville in 1942 and the National Institutes of Health nearby 11 years later. In recent years the area has become a cosmopolitan downtown with a multinational population, including many retirees or

young singles, thriving hotels, shops, restaurants, luxury high-rise condominiums, and more than 11 million square feet of high-rise and mid-rise office space.

Years before the Civil War, a settlement grew near a crossroads where clear, fresh water bubbled up through a bed of sand laced with glittering mica. Named, appropriately, Silver Spring, the community became a waystation on northern turnpikes, and, later, a stop on the railroad and electric trolley lines.

Home to several prominent county citizens, Silver Spring was a choice suburban homesite for the expanding federal work force between World Wars I and II. With the arrival of Metro service in the 1980s, its downtown business district, much of it built 50 years before, has been the scene of substantial redevelopment. The best of this reflects or preserves the district's art deco and moderne style, while adding high-rise offices and mixed-use centers to

Youngsters at a Bethesda church come together to work on a community project. High-rise condos and shopping centers now line Bethesda's urban corridors; side streets still have that hometown feeling. Photo by Jim Pickerell/Folio

Rockville's high-tech developments contrast sharply with its Victorian historic district. Photo by Robert Rathe/ Folio

growth and home of its government's new Upcounty Center.

Germantown is part of the I-270 corridor, a suburban-urban phenomenon that may well be Montgomery County's downtown of the future. A giant swath encompassing Rockville, Gaithersburg, and Germantown and continuing across the border into Frederick, the I-270 corridor is the site of the county's leading-edge business development. It is also the scene of a substantial part of its population growth—accounting for almost 40 percent of the households established countywide since 1980.

Anchored by key federal research and development facilities such as the National Institutes of Health (NIH), the National Oceanic and Atmospheric Administration (NOAA), the Food and Drug Administration (FDA), in and around Rockville; the National Institute of Standards and Technology (NIST, formerly the Bureau of Standards) in Gaithersburg; and the Department of Energy's Energy Research and Development Administration (ERDA) in Germantown, the I-270 corridor claims one of the highest concentrations of high-tech industries in the United States.

Not surprisingly, more scientists and engineers live and work in the I-270 corridor, per capita, than in virtually any other U.S. urban area. The corridor is the main reason why Montgomery County leads the state in high-tech employment, with more than one-third of Maryland's scientists and technicians—more than 35,000 people—working here.

Many of the scientists who commute to jobs along the state-of-the-art, 12-lane highway work in the fast-growing field of biotechnology. Here, behind the postmodern pediments and neo-deco

The latest technology is used to track weather systems at the National Oceanic and Atmospheric Administration lab in Rockville. NOAA is one of many state-of-the-art research facilities in Montgomery County. Photo by Greg Pease

the busy streetscape.

Wheaton, where an eighteenth-century tavern served travelers heading west to Bladensburg and north to Brookeville, today stands at the heart of the county's suburban growth. In recent years that growth has concentrated in high-density corridors anticipating the completion of the final phase of Metro's Red Line, which opened as far as Wheaton in 1990. Far to the northwest, Germantown is the focus of the county's newest suburban

curtainwalls of more than 15 million square feet of offices and R & D labs, they create the products of tomorrow: more accurate AIDS tests, disease-resistant strains of crops, safer and more effective pharmaceuticals, as well as the reagents and equipment needed to support them.

A billion-dollar industry today, biotechnology is expected to mushroom to close to $40 billion annually within

the next 10 years as new products emerge from the lengthy federal approvals process and onto the market. For example, analysts estimate that by 1995, 50 percent of all pharmaceuticals will be direct or indirect products of biotechnology. After California, Maryland has the largest concentration of biotechnology firms in the United States, with two-thirds of those located within Montgomery County. Firms here

Dramatic new glass-and-steel office towers reflect a multinational population. Photo by Greg Pease

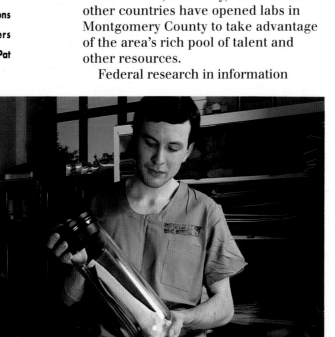

have attracted capital from around the world; and companies from Japan, Great Britain, Germany, and several other countries have opened labs in Montgomery County to take advantage of the area's rich pool of talent and other resources.

Federal research in information technology, along with the continuing needs of the Department of Defense and other agencies, have encouraged more than 150 computer software, hardware, and services companies in the county. Many of these are also located in the I-270 corridor. To spur the industry, Montgomery County's High Technology Council, a public-private partnership coordinated by the Office of Economic Development, has received a state grant to take the first steps toward creating a Maryland Information Technologies Center where business, government, and universities would coordinate research in cutting-edge fields such as fiber optics and digital switching systems. The council, whose 230 members represent more than 50,000 employees, has already created a varied menu of practical resources for the industry, including seminars and breakfast programs through Information and Biotechnology Networks and ED-LINK, a computer bulletin board of high-tech education opportunities available to industry practitioners and citizens.

The High Technology Council has been the keystone of the remarkable cooperative effort by county, state, education, and industry that created the Shady Grove Life Sciences Center near Rockville. Centerpiece of the I-270 corridor, the 288-acre campus is home to educational and research facilities of Johns Hopkins University and the University of Maryland as well as several private biotech firms. To attract this prestigious resource for its biotech industry, Montgomery County provided more than $40 million in land, roads, and buildings plus an incalculable amount in knowhow and enthusiastic leadership.

At Shady Grove, Johns Hopkins University's Montgomery County Center offers nine graduate-degree programs in engineering and computer sciences, management, and public health and

presently serves about 1,100 students. The University of Maryland's Shady Grove Campus will offer technology and business management courses to about 3,000 graduate and upper-level undergraduate students in a new classroom facility scheduled to be completed early in 1992.

Scientists at the University of Maryland's Center for Advanced Research in Biotechnology (CARB) are already exploring research frontiers that have passed beyond genetic engineering to the direct manipulation of protein structures themselves. The results of this research advance such diverse human needs as immune therapy and waste management. A joint effort of Maryland's state university system, the National Institute of Standards and Technology, and Montgomery County, CARB is widely praised as a prototype of cooperation at three governmental levels. Likewise, the Shady Grove Life Sciences Center is intended to promote a synergistic relationship among researchers, educators, and industry to achieve their mutual goals.

Of the estimated 20,500 private businesses in Montgomery County, just a dozen or so employ more than 1,500 people; 97 percent—including most of the high-tech firms—were classified as "small." Entrepreneurs in search of professional development opportunities can choose from seminars, workshops, and programs offered by many business and governmental organizations.

Montgomery College, the county's highly regarded community college system, offers 50 technical-degree programs and hundreds of continuing-education courses in industry-related fields; and the Small Business Development Center in Bethesda offers important start-up and growth-management resources. Technology and product development assistance is available through technical assistance programs offered by the University of Maryland, including its Maryland Industrial Partnerships and its Technology Extension Service. Federal research laboratories in the county, such as NIH and NIST, are also important resources for local businesses.

The spectacular growth that swept through the Potomac region in the 1980s transformed much of Montgomery County's landscape as well as its community life. Both the county's population and its at-place employment jumped by about 150,000 between 1980 and 1990.

At Bethesda's Metro Centre and stations down the line, the Metrorail rapid transit system has pushed urban development far into Montgomery County. Photo by Michael Ventura/Folio

With 455,000 jobs, Montgomery County is the metro area's largest suburban employment center. Thanks to the 1980s trend toward "privatization," which sent many federal programs to non-governmental contractors, the private sector now provides about 82 percent of the jobs in the county, a jump of 49 percent since 1980. The county's 19 federal agencies had some 42,000 people on their combined payrolls as of 1989.

Most of Montgomery County's work force is now employed within the county, a trend that is increasing; and today more than two-fifths of those workers go to jobs outside the beltway, reversing

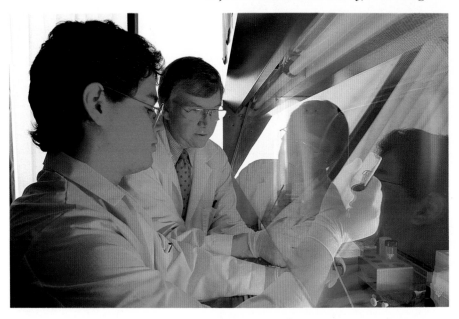

commuting patterns of years past. To support the needs of these workers, almost 20 million square feet of office and R&D space was constructed during the building boom of the 1980s. During the subsequent economic slowdown, Montgomery County office buildings generally displayed fewer "Vacancy" signs than those in some of its suburban neighbors.

Most analysts believe that Montgomery County's era as a commuter suburb for Washington, D.C., is now over. Just in time for the twenty-first century, America's suburb is becoming a new kind of all-American hometown.

There is still some controversy about how that town of the future will look. The county extends an enthusiastic hand to commercial growth through the Office of Economic Development, which looks ahead to the year 2020 with the slogan, "Making Our Future Your

Business." On the other hand, leading citizens and business representatives serving on the county's Commission on the Future recently recommended that the rate of new residential construction should be doubled, and the rate of new jobs should be cut in half to balance the effects of recent expansion. In 1990's countywide election, the pro-development policies of incumbent County Executive Sidney Kramer were challenged by the slow-growth platform of challenger Neil Potter. Potter won.

Potter grew up on a Montgomery

Nostalgia is the daily special at Vintage Diner in Chevy Chase. A turn-of-the-century luxury housing project, the area grew rapidly in the 1940s and 1950s. Photo by Joseph Sohm/Chromosohm

County farm that now lies mostly under an on-ramp for the Capital Beltway. In recent years other family farms have been saved from similar incursions of progress by several county programs that relieve tax pressures and otherwise make it economically feasible for farmland to remain in production. So far the various plans have protected about 31,000 of the 100,000 acres of farmland remaining in Montgomery County, and additional land is acquired at the rate of about 1,000 acres per year. Meanwhile the county's agriculture industry continues to produce an annual yield of nearly $170 million. Crops include landscape and ornamental plants, along with grain, vegetables, and horses.

Montgomery County has recently developed an Agricultural History Farm Park to recall the family farms that once

spread across this gently pitched land. Other historic sites combine preservation programs with the arts, contributing to the cultural identity that the county increasingly claims as its own.

Strathmore Hall Arts Center is a Georgian-style mansion that occupies a hill not far from downtown Rockville. Since it was built in 1902, it has been home to a succession of prominent families, among these, the President of the Philippines, who took refuge there during World War II. Montgomery County has refurbished the glowing wood panels and marble carvings, creating a refined setting for concerts, ethnic festivals, art exhibitions, and afternoon teatime recitals. Downtown, Rockville Arts Place, which includes members' galleries, gallery space, and artists' studios, provides a creatively contrasting environment for contemporary arts.

For 14 seasons the county has also been impresario of the Round House Theatre, named for its home in a recycled elementary school, whose resident Equity company presents a full season of mainstage plays, children's theater, and special events. Critics consistently praise Round House offerings, which feature new plays and new writers as well as a smattering of the classics. Montgomery is the only county government in the nation that runs its own professional theater.

The City of Rockville is equally proud of its Civic Center Mansion, a 1926 neoclassical plantation-style house, which is the centerpiece of a 100-acre complex of performing and recreational facilities. A gallery in the mansion itself exhibits the work of local and regional artists. Also on the grounds is the contemporary, 500-seat F. Scott Fitzgerald Theatre, named for one of the city's most famous sons.

Chipped into the headstone of Fitzgerald's grave in a cemetery nearby, his words speak wearily of civilization: "So we beat on, boats against the current, borne back ceaselessly into the past." Today in Montgomery County progress itself flows westward into the

The C&O Canal, built to traverse the Potomac's rapids and realize George Washington's vision, is a now a National Historical Park that runs along Montgomery County's southern border, a few feet above the river itself. In George-town and at the Visitor's Center at Great Falls, families can ride mule-towed barges through restored locks that take them stairstep-wise upriver by the same ingenious mechanics that worked just fine in the nineteenth century. Farther west the park turns into a trail, hidden by giant oaks and sycamores from highway traffic and the architect-designed homes that command the palisades nearby.

Here, where deer and raccoon still make surprise appearances through the brush, and the sun sets through the leaves slant by slant, Montgomery County is both a reality and a memory. In the eyes of many of its citizens, that's the good life at its best.

Above and left: Following the Potomac for 184.5 miles from Georgetown to Cumberland, Maryland, the C&O Canal was begun in 1828 to open trade with the west. Supreme Court Justice William O. Douglas led successful efforts to make the route a National Historical Park. Top photo by Bob Rowan/Progressive Image Photography; inset photo by Joseph Sohm/Chromosohm

progress itself flows westward into the highlands, borne on the giant surge of commerce that has carried the Washing-ton statistical metropolitan area all the way out to West Virginia.

Two hundred years ago, George Washington looked past the giant cataracts of the Potomac River and saw a corridor for trade with the West. A businessman long before he became a soldier or a politician, he believed that the new capital must be a center of commerce as well. So Washington es-tablished his namesake here, where the white water mellowed into the tidal port of Georgetown at the forward edge of Montgomery County.

Chapter Four

FAIRFAX COUNTY, VIRGINIA

New Towns, New Cities

Metrorail zips over Northern Virginia's hills past rush hour commuters on I-66. Photo by Cameron Davidson/Folio

In a rapidly growing region, Fairfax County has bloomed fastest of all. Twenty years ago it was a sedate suburb with plenty of rural countryside that its most famous son, George Washington, would have found familiar. Today it is a regional metropolis with a population that has nearly doubled, from 454,275 in 1970 to 815,223 in 1990. Between 1980 and 1990, when people poured into the county at the rate of about 20,000 a year, the 399 square miles of Fairfax County absorbed more than half of the growth in the metropolitan Washington area and just less than two-thirds of the increase in Northern Virginia.

Fairfax County's growth is the natural progression of development outward from the District of Columbia that began with the New Deal and World War II. During the 1950s the boom reached Fairfax County when thousands of government workers, who found the quiet suburbs of Arlington too confining, headed for the wide-open spaces across the county line.

Sheer numbers, though, have lately changed the landscape like a video played at fast forward. Virtually overnight, Victorian villages have been transformed into bustling suburban centers and entire new towns have sprung from woods where the tracks of deer and beaver were still fresh in the earth. Most dramatic of all is the development

Lord Thomas Fairfax, proprietor of the Northern Neck of Virginia, distributed generous land grants to those who would pay for the land, settle it, and plant it. Painting by Sir Joshua Reynolds. Courtesy, Alexandria-Washington Lodge No.22. From Cirker, *Dictionary of American Portraits*

Far right: Lawyer and planter William Fitzhugh (1651-1701) once held patents to more than 50,000 acres in Fairfax County. Painting by Gustavus Hasselius. From Cirker, *Dictionary of American Portraits*

of Tyson's Corner, a "downtown in the suburbs," with more office space than center city Seattle, San Diego, Fort Worth, or Cincinnati. This commercial center has materialized at the spot where a single general store sat on a quiet country crossroads not quite 30 years ago.

Driving past the glass-and-steel hotels, office parks, and shopping centers stacked beside every highway, one finds it difficult to imagine that, until recently, much of Fairfax County's land was sparsely settled and unused.

Once part of the 5.2-million-acre tract controlled by the sixth Lord Fairfax, this uppermost portion of the Northern Neck was the last of Virginia's Tidewater to be colonized. To encourage development, Lord Fairfax, like other Virginia proprietors, gave generous land grants to encourage settlement of the area.

Enterprising grantees quickly amassed giant holdings of their own. William Fitzhugh, Robert E. Lee's forebear, at one time held patents to more than 50,000 acres. Landholders were offered bounties of additional acreage to recruit other settlers; and squatters who farmed land without the benefit of a patent were rarely evicted.

By 1742, when the county was incorporated, its economy was dominated by great tobacco plantations that lined the main waterways. The Washington family owned 5,000 acres on the Potomac that they called Mt. Vernon. Nearby was

Gunston Hall, the freehold of Washington's good friend and fellow patriot, George Mason, who later was known as the "Father of the Bill of Rights." These estates were farmed by large forces of slave labor, smaller farms were worked by their owners with little help. Roads were scarred and rudimentary, used mostly to roll huge hogshead barrels of tobacco to the port towns of Alexandria on the Potomac and Colchester on the Occoquan River.

Tobacco farming by the profligate plantation method proved to be disastrous to the soil. In the early days of the new republic, Virginia planters experimented with other crops in hopes of saving their economy. But it was already too late. In his 1787 *Notes on the State of Virginia,* Thomas Jefferson, an avid scientific farmer, observed that the amount of manure needed to coax wheat from local soil cost more than the crop would bring at market. As a result of these soil conditions, the great estates were sold

off piecemeal, and soon even the pieces were abandoned.

Traveling through the once-flourishing Virginia countryside in 1842, Charles Dickens described it as "little better than a sandy desert overgrown with trees."

A wave of settlers from the north, who

began arriving in the decade before the Civil War, began to rejuvenate the land with new agricultural techniques and a work ethic based on free, rather than slave, labor. Former Indian trails evolved into market highways, and small communities, including Fairfax City and Falls Church, grew at the intersections. Railroad lines made it convenient for federal workers to commute from close-in villages such as Vienna and to escape the summer heat in Victorian vacation towns such as Herndon in the Blue Ridge mountain foothills and Clifton in the lush south county woods.

1791 surveyors for the new District of Columbia placed its western borders against the eastern edge of Falls Church. Although that portion of the District was later returned to Virginia, the adjacent city of Falls Church became one of the capital region's earliest suburbs. Falls Church today is a well-established and populous community, home to government workers, military families, young professionals, recent immigrants, and local merchants.

A little crossroads known as Earp's Corner, first settled in the early 1700s, was renamed Providence when the

The city of Fairfax was called Fairfax Courthouse for a while after the county seat was located there in 1800. The courthouse lawn was the scene of the only Civil War battle on county soil, a skirmish with Mosby's Raiders. Photo by Joseph Sohm/ Chromosohm

Successive improvements in transportation—a suburban trolley, the Capital Beltway, other interstate highways, Metrorail, and, most recently, the commuter toll highway to Dulles International Airport—have carried waves of new settlers to the county's outer limits. Byways only recently rural are now the main streets of pleasant suburban cities and towns that spread over the county's hills.

Just west of the Fairfax County line is the site of the county's second parish church, which was built in 1733 at the intersection of Leesburg Pike and the road to the Little Falls of the Potomac. The settlement, appropriately named Falls Church, became a meeting place for prominent county landowners. In

county courthouse was built there in 1800. That tiny town has grown into the independent City of Fairfax, with a population of about 20,000. The red-brick courthouse is still the centerpiece of the city's Colonial downtown, while nearby stand a concrete-and-glass judicial center and the high-rise Massey Building, which houses many of Fairfax County's administrative offices. Down the road is the 583-acre main campus of George Mason University.

Vienna, a farm community that blossomed in the 1900s when a trolley line whisked commuters into the District, is a quiet, family neighborhood of large homes with big backyards. It is located just a mile south of Tyson's Corner, the county's biggest commercial development.

Vienna is bordered by two of the county's most exclusive communities: Oakton, a hilly enclave of horse farms and contemporary estates, and McLean, a discreet grande dame of a community that is also a neighbor to the headquarters of the Central Intelligence Agency.

Annandale, which was once part of the 24,000-acre Ravensworth Plantation, was resettled in the 1850s by a Mennonite family from Pennsylvania, who established a post office and blacksmith shop there. During the Civil War, Union soldiers destroyed the town's Methodist church, but citizens rebuilt it. Today Annandale is a mature suburb and home to active and retired federal workers as well as a growing local business base.

The first prominent citizen of Bailey's Crossroads was Hachaliah Bailey, who bought 500 acres of land there in 1837 to use as a winter home for his "Zoological Institute" (later known as the Barnum & Bailey Circus). In the 1950s nearby Seven Corners became home to the area's first regional shopping center, which is the nucleus of a busy commercial intersection at Leesburg and Columbia Pikes.

George Washington's old neighborhood near Mt. Vernon remains one of the county's most desirable places to live. Among the fine residences overlooking the Potomac River are carefully preserved historic houses, including Woodlawn Plantation, once home to Martha Washington's granddaughter, Nelly Custis Lewis, and the Pope-Leighey House, one of Frank Lloyd Wright's prototypical "Unsonian" homes. Both properties are now owned by the National Trust for Historic Preservation. Farther south Fort Belvoir, named for the plantation home built by a cousin of Lord Fairfax, is a quiet community of military and civilian residents.

Burke is a residential area growing up among the lakes and woods in southern Fairfax County. Nearby are located the planned community of Burke Centre

and new home developments near the historic rail depot at Fairfax Station. Lorton, at the county's southernmost tip, is a quiet, well-established neighborhood with many young families. It is close to both I-95 and the playgrounds of Pohick Bay Regional Park. With freshly painted white porches and gardens brimming with petunias, Clifton, remains as pretty as a Victorian picture postcard.

On the hills and in the valleys bordering the Potomac, Great Falls, in the northwest corner of Fairfax County, is home to many of the county's most elegant estates. Nearby Mather Gorge in Great Falls Park is the site of some of the county's most dramatic natural landscape.

The 7,200 acres of west county woodland that became Reston was purchased in 1898 by a German physician named Carl Wiehle who wanted to build a utopian community. His effort failed, but more than 60 years later another visionary developer, Robert E. Simon, tried again. A product of imaginative county zoning, which allows Reston and similar communities to offer a variety of living and working choices while preserving open space, Reston today combines a new urban Town Center, a high-tech office corridor, and hundreds of acres of parkland with townhouses, single-family homes, apartments, and condos for more than 65,000 people.

Nearby, the town of Herndon, a nineteenth-century railroad town that became a twentieth-century agricultural center, approaches the year 2000 as a prime location for high-tech and aerospace industries. At the center of town, gracious Queen Anne homes still stand on wide, well-tended green lawns; and Herndon's Victorian downtown has become a popular arts, shopping, and restaurant district.

Despite this modest early development, Fairfax County remained primarily a rural outpost and bedroom community for commuters to the District of

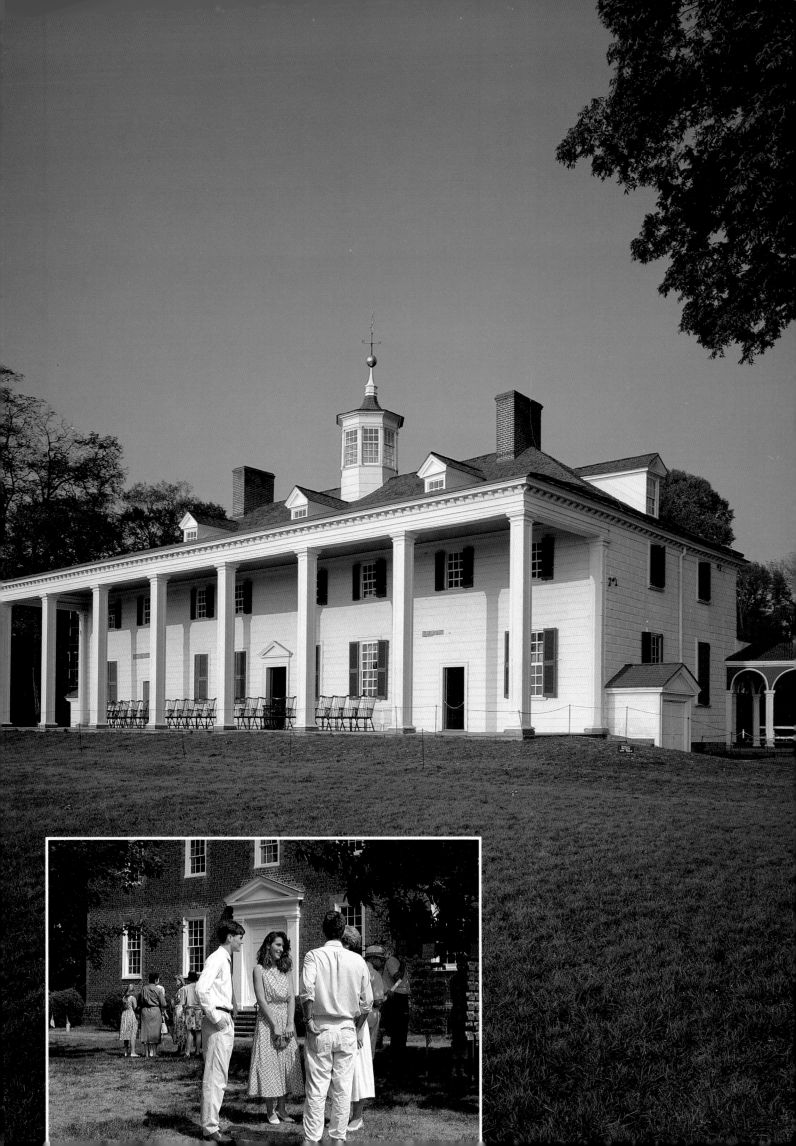

Columbia until the mid-1970s. Then, recalls longtime northern Virginia businessman and land-use planner Sidney O. Dewberry, "The area suddenly reached critical mass. It began to stand on its own, independent of Washington, D.C."

In addition to businesses meant to service the federal government or the affluent suburban market, new firms began to locate here "just because it is a nice place to live and work," says Dewberry, who moved his own engineering and architectural firm, Dewberry & Davis, to the Merrifield area in 1965. Business also took notice of the county's well-educated work force and attracted more of the same. An astonishing 95.8 percent of the county's adult residents over the age of 25 are high school graduates, and 55 percent have gone on to finish at least four years of college.

The county's growth in this era has transformed it into a suburban metropolis where new high-rise downtowns occupy hills just recently home to dairy cattle and wildflowers. From 1970 to 1980 about 1.25 million square feet of office space was built in Fairfax County each year, bringing the inventory to 17.6 million square feet and creating almost 100,000 new jobs at decade's end. Fueled by the region's overall economic prosperity, growth in the 1980s continued its geometric progression: doubling to 34.8 million square feet between 1980 and 1985, then nearly doubling again to 61.2 million square feet in 1989. The Fairfax County Economic Development Authority estimates that in 1990 there were 366,000 jobs in the county, almost 80 percent of them in white-collar occupations. Not surprisingly, Fairfax County has been experiencing a period of much slower growth as demand for available space catches up with supply. As the end of the nationwide recession nears, however, the streets and sidewalks of these highly desirable locations are once more beginning to bustle.

Almost one-third of Fairfax County's new office buildings are in Tyson's Corner. Adjoining the historic town of

Vienna and the affluent suburb of McLean, the 1,700-acre urban center occupies, fittingly, the highest hills in Fairfax County and overlooks its major transportation arteries—the Capitol Beltway, I-66, Route 123, Leesburg Pike, and the Dulles Access Highway. Almost 100,000 people are employed in the postmodern high rises and luxury office parks, where firms specializing in

computers, software, communications, and other high-tech endeavors do business with the U.S. government and the rest of the world.

Convenient to both Capitol Hill and Dulles Airport, Tyson's is home to several corporate headquarters as well as to national associations as diverse as the National Wildlife Federation and the National Automobile Dealers Association. To support this community, Tyson's has also attracted an impressive cadre of professional services: major law and accounting firms, management and technical consultants, suppliers of communications equipment and systems, plus more than a dozen major commercial banks. Twenty hotels, including the luxury Sheraton Premiere and a brand new Ritz Carlton provide almost 4,000 rooms and suites (about 40 percent of the county's inventory). Tyson's is also one of the East Coast's premiere retail centers with eight

Facing page: Privileged ponies graze in Oakton's wide, rolling pastures, just a mile or two from the corporate offices ranked along the booming I-66 corridor. Photo by Carol Highsmith Photography

Above: A deliveryman for the Great Falls Ice Company shows off a large block of the frozen substance to a group of capital region schoolchildren in 1899. Courtesy, Library of Congress, Prints and Photographs Division

Whitewater thunders through Mather Gorge below the Great Falls of the Potomac. The Washington area produces and trains several of the nation's top Olympic canoe and kayak competitors. Background photo by Greg Pease; inset photo by Carol Highsmith Photography

top-of-the-line department store chains, including Neiman Marcus, Saks Fifth Avenue, Lord & Taylor, and Bloomingdale's, plus hundreds of specialty stores in the giant Tyson's Corner and Tyson's II malls and a dozen nearby shopping centers. Not surprisingly, when Fairfax County's business community formed its first private club, Tyson's Corner was the natural choice for its home.

Growth just as dramatic has lately come to the western edge of the county along the Dulles Access Road between Reston and Herndon, creating a powerful high-tech corridor from meadows and woods.

From the beginning, Reston's campus-like office parks and open spaces made the new town a compatible home to educational and trade associations as well as to computer services, communications, and technical R&D firms. Since 1987, when the National Aeronautics and Space Administration (NASA) selected Reston as headquarters for its program to design and launch its first orbiting space station, the area has become even more desirable. Even as Congress debates its future, NASA's multibillion-dollar space station project has attracted dozens of allied enterprises to Reston, whose inventory of premium office space has jumped to nearly 10 million square feet.

At the edge of neighboring Loudoun County, a couple of miles west, the dramatic black-and-silver trapezoidal tower of the Center for Innovative Technology (CIT) serves notice that the Victorian town of Herndon is looking forward, not back. Created by the Commonwealth of Virginia as a catalyst for the development, dissemination, and application of new technologies, CIT has provided a spark to Virginia business and has brought substantial corporate funding to research programs at the state's universities. Adjoining CIT is the Software Productivity Consortium.

Facing page: **Mostly woods and fields 20 years ago, the new town of Reston is nearing a population of 75,000. The Reston-Dulles corridor has more office buildings than many big U.S. cities. Photo by Carol Highsmith Photography**

Above and left: **Young and old alike enjoy the festivities at Reston Town Center, a high-tech office corridor with parkland and residential areas. Photos by Larry Ghiorsi/ Brooklyn Image Group**

First-class hotels and conference centers serve Tyson's Corner's expansive business community and cut a dramatic skyline across the Blue Ridge foothills. Photo by Robert Llewellyn

With a membership roster that reads like a Who's Who of aerospace, aviation, and defense technology, SPC develops advanced software for applications in federal systems and high-tech industry.

Dozens of international companies are also attracted to the Reston-Herndon area because of its proximity to Dulles International Airport just across the border in Loudoun County. The nation's first jetport, Dulles is now in the midst of a multimillion-dollar capital improvement and expansion program. As the region's primary air-cargo center, Dulles has become even more attractive to international business now that it has a Foreign Trade Zone (where imported products and components can be assembled and reshipped, bypassing customs).

Convenient to I-66, Tyson's Corner, and the city of Fairfax, Fairfax Center has become another fast-growing location for business, with more than 4 million square feet of office space in use and more in development. Spacious and upscale, the area offers access to an important transportation corridor and a pristine, wooded setting. That combination has proved irresistible to several

prestigious corporations, including giant Mobil Corporation, which has made Fairfax Center home to its sleek, new international headquarters. Fairfax County's gleaming new government center complex here will be the heart of its administrative and program operations.

Nearby Merrifield is an important multipurpose commercial area whose convenient location has made it a center for regional facilities such the 665-bed Fairfax Hospital (the county's biggest) and the Northern Virginia Sectional Center Facility of the United States Postal Service.

Light industry continues to thrive along the I-95 corridor in Springfield and Newington. Once part of a vast plantation called Ravenswood, which was a summer retreat for the Robert E. Lee family, this south county area was the site of Fairfax County's early manufacturing activity. It was linked to markets north and south by rail and by one of the nation's first superhighways. Today the region is home to a diverse base of manufacturers, wholesale distributors and warehouses, and technical services, construction, and utility firms.

Throughout the county growth in business has been accompanied by an increasing share of the kind of resources that make communities pleasant places to live.

Fairfax County's public school system, with 128,000 students, is now the 10th largest in the nation as well as one of the best. High school seniors consistently average 70 to 80 points above national and state averages on the standardized Scholastic Aptitude Test.

Public school programs accommodate the needs of a population that is both growing and changing. More than 4,000 children from 126 countries are enrolled in the ESL (English as a Second Language) Program, and a dozen different special education programs address the specific learning needs of some 16,000 children. Enrichment programs are available for "gifted and talented" students from third grade through high school, and the Thomas Jefferson High School of Science and Technology (with state-of-the-art equipment supplied, in part, by local business) is a magnet for some of the county's brightest young minds. George C. Marshall High School offers programs ranging from computer programming to cosmetology to advanced vocational training.

In elementary schools a before- and after-class child care program provides a vital service in a county where almost 75 percent of the women (many of them mothers of school-age children) work outside of the home.

Probably no single institution mirrors the county's growth as dramatically as George Mason University. Less than 30 years ago it served a small suburban community as a two-year extension of the University of Virginia, with a tiny four-building campus, 28 faculty members, and 36 students. Today's GMU is rapidly outgrowing its 90-building campus near the City of Fairfax. Independent since 1972, the university now offers more than 100 baccalaureate and post-graduate degree programs, including the nation's first doctorates in conflict resolution and information technology. The student population, which grew by 72.5 percent between 1980 and 1990, now tops 19,000 and accounts for nearly 40 percent of the enrollment of the state's six doctoral-level universities.

GMU's increase in size has been accompanied by a commensurate increase in the quality, effectiveness, and sophistication of its curriculum. Since 1981 SAT scores of incoming freshmen have risen 100 points; their average is now more than 150 points above the average score for freshmen nationally. In the five years from 1983 to 1988, research grants to the university jumped from $3.2 million to $25.1 million. During that same period the number of endowed professorships rose from one to 16.

Worldwide attention came to GMU in 1987, when Dr. James M. Buchanan, who holds the university's first endowed chair, was awarded the Nobel Prize in economics. A $12-million, 2,000-seat concert hall is the much-acclaimed centerpiece of the George Mason Center for the Arts. Opened in September 1990, the facility offers a public performance series with well-known pop and classical artists and casts a limelight on music, dance, and theater activities throughout the county.

Meanwhile Northern Virginia Community College has forged productive alliances with local industry, providing general and job-specific vocational training and professional development at NOVA's Annandale Campus and other sites throughout the county.

Overlooking Fountain Square, a new high-rise Hyatt Regency Hotel is a focal point of Reston's new Town Center. With murals by noted artist Jacques Lamy, the hotel's Cafe Allegro is a popular local dining spot. Photo by Joseph Sohm/Chromosohm

Despite the building boom, natural areas and wide open spaces are usually within gazing distance, even in the most urbanized areas of Fairfax County. Right in the midst of Tyson's Corner, office workers can slip away for lakeside brown-bag lunches among the azaleas at Meadowlark Gardens Regional Park, the area's newest. As a matter of fact, Fairfax County has over 50 percent more acres of parks than all of its office, industrial, and retail land combined. During the county's great spurt of commercial growth from 1975 to 1990, parkland was added at almost double the rate of commercial/industrial acreage.

At the county's southern border, a chain of parks that lines the Occoquan River and Bull Run Creek offers marinas, ball fields, nature trails, and thousands of acres of wilderness while providing a buffer zone between the region's water supply and nearby development. Farther east on the Occoquan, the 2,277-acre Mason Neck Wildlife Refuge is an important nesting habitat for a growing flock of endangered bald eagles.

An evening of opera, bluegrass, or classic rock 'n' roll under the stars is all the incentive most people need to visit Wolf Trap Farm Park in Vienna, the nation's only National Park for the performing arts. Picnic dinners are encouraged. Smaller programs, including children's theater and jazz, are presented year round in The Barns at Wolf Trap.

Other parks preserve sites from the area's rich history. For example, Sully, near Dulles International Airport, is a plantation built in 1794 that has had its main house, dependencies, and grounds restored and is now open for tours. At Colvin Run Mill schoolchildren can watch corn being ground by a giant water-driven stone wheel, and their folks can buy brown bags of cornmeal to make into muffins according to the original recipe.

The Potomac River crashes down 80 feet through a series of cascades into Mather Gorge at Great Falls Park. When his 1607 exploration was halted by the rapids just downstream, Captain John Smith described the spectacle: "Mighty rocks growing above the ground as high as the shrub . . . places where the waters

Poised for flight, Eero Saarinen's main terminal building at Dulles International Airport is an unforgettable gateway to the capital region. The Concorde is a regular visitor. Photo by Carol Highsmith Photography

had fallen from the high mountain . . . 'spangled scurf' that made many bare places seem as gilded." A company founded by George Washington in 1785 developed the Patowmack Canal to bypass the falls and open trade with the west. Parts of the canal have been restored, and nearby stand some stone walls, hearths, and chimneys from the village of Matildaville, whose residents tended the canal until the 1820s. (Incidentally, the "spangled scurf" that Captain Smith noticed was probably gold since there once was a gold mine at Matildaville.)

The centerpiece of the county's history—and tourism—is Mt. Vernon, George Washington's estate in the county's southeastern corner. The Mount Vernon Ladies' Association has carefully restored the property with many of the family's own belongings and has preserved home, furnishings, and gardens with great care and beauty.

Thanks to the federal, Commonwealth, and local authorities, the land surrounding Mt. Vernon is maintained as parks and wilderness so visitors can enjoy the same view across the Potomac

that the first President savored more than 250 years ago. Nearby Gunston Hall has also been restored with the formal Georgian furnishings and gardens favored by George Mason.

While Fairfax County residents are undeniably high achievers, prosperity is hardly their only priority. In a rapidly changing world, newcomers and old settlers look to their communities for a sense of continuity and place, and they are willing to work hard to achieve it. That's why executives, teachers, sales clerks, and bureaucrats hurry home from work, grab a bite to eat, and rush off again to contribute their talents to the Springfield Community Theatre, the Reston Chorale, or any one of more than 100 other community-based performing arts groups in the county. Several of these have become so expert and sophisticated that it is increasingly difficult

At Wolf Trap Farm Park, patrons can watch the show from under the roof of the open-air Filene Center or bring a blanket and sit on the lawn outside. Picnic dinners are optional. Photo by Carol Highsmith Photography

Facing page: Built in 1811, Colvin Run Mill, near Great Falls, is a remnant of the days when corn and wheat were the county's leading cash crops. Restored to working order, it's a county park. Photo by Ken Heinen

to distinguish their work from that of professional organizations downtown.

Premiere among these is the Fairfax Symphony. In 1957 the orchestra performed four concerts a year for an audience of friends and neighbors in the auditorium of a local high school. Now, under the baton of Music Director William Hudson, they perform for 100,000 people a year on the area's top stages, including the Kennedy Center. Subscription concerts often feature internationally known guest soloists and earn glowing reviews, even from hard-to-impress downtown critics.

Sports also benefit from broad-based community participation. Most towns

Bicyclists and joggers make good use of the paved trail that follows the route of the former Washington and Old Dominion Railroad, once an important commuter route through the country from the Blue Ridge to the Potomac. Photo by Carol Highsmith Photography

have active Little League baseball teams, and youth soccer has become an obsession in communities countywide. High school football and basketball games are often sellouts, especially at state and metro-area tournaments, where local teams are known as powerful competitors. Joggers fill suburban roads before and after working hours, and bicyclists like the traffic-free W & OD Railroad Regional Park, an abandoned right of way that has been paved over as a recreational trail.

Touching every aspect of life, the dramatic growth that Fairfax County has experienced inevitably brings problems.

Yet citizens, government, and business have found common ground on their way to finding solutions.

Concerned that rising land prices are forcing an important segment of the county's work force to live outside the county, Fairfax County's Board of Supervisors, in cooperation with builders and community leaders, passed an affordable housing ordinance that encourages production of moderately priced housing in exchange for density variances.

Aware that Fairfax County's wooded landscape, clean air, and open sky are among its greatest assets, the Board of Supervisors has adopted goals that confirm its commitment to protecting the natural environment and preserving open space. Equally aware that the county's environment helps attract a first-class work force, most designers and developers cooperate by creating residential and commercial projects with substantial open space and imaginative environmental buffers, even in high-density areas. And noting that most residents now commute to work within the county, planners agree with often-gridlocked drivers that Fairfax County has one thing in common with its Colonial days—the roads still need improvement.

Public/private partnerships have proposed some innovative solutions to the county's transportation needs. Recent ideas have included a privately funded light rail line to Dulles Airport, as well as the continuing program of builder-funded transportation improvements that integrate new developments into existing traffic systems.

New transportation corridors such as these will probably be ready just in time to carry twenty-first century settlers to points even farther out along the metropolitan frontier. Until then, commuters counting the seconds until the traffic light turns green can look up and over the nearby hills and relish the landscape that made a westward-looking visionary of George Washington. In the midst of growth and change, Fairfax County is still a beautiful place to live.

Chapter Five

PRINCE GEORGE'S COUNTY, MARYLAND

. . . .

County at the Crossroads

P rince George's County has always occupied a favored place in the capital region. Fewer than 10 miles inland of Chesapeake Bay, it is bounded by two great tidal rivers, the Patuxent on the east and the Potomac on the west; in between, its 489 square miles of sandy lowlands are threaded with a dozen feeders and tributaries. Above the Potomac, Prince George's shares 17 miles of border with Washington, D.C. Through Prince George's northern corner, it is a short, straight ride to Baltimore and from there to the great commercial centers of Philadelphia, New York, and Boston.

In 1800 Abigail Adams made the journey down the road through Prince George's from Baltimore with an entourage of 10 to join her husband in the barely completed White House. The road being little more than an Indian trail, the group soon got lost. The First Lady later recalled "wandering more than two hours in the woods in different paths, holding down and breaking boughs of trees which we could not pass," until a "solitary black fellow with a horse and cart kindly offered to conduct us."

The old road is now US 1, and motorists can drive from Baltimore to Washington in less than an hour. If they

Interpreters at the National Colonial Farm demonstrate what life was like in the capital region before Washington, D.C., was established. Many of the region's best-preserved Colonial manor houses and churches are in Prince George's County. Photo by Carol Highsmith Photography

prefer, they can zip back and forth on Amtrak's *Metroliner* or on one of the MARC commuter rail trains that follow the same route through Prince George's County. Regionally, more than 40 miles of the Capital Beltway tie Prince George's to Washington, D.C., Montgomery County, and Virginia; and a neat system of radial highways brings the Beltway within a pleasant drive of virtually every corner of the county.

This regional accessibility has made Prince George's County's position more favorable than ever as Washington, D.C.,

and Baltimore merge into a single metropolitan market. Visionaries see the northern part of the county as a high-tech swath in which government, higher education, and business draw freely from the resources in both cities to create the enterprises of tomorrow: supercomputing, biotechnology, space exploration, and even twenty-first century agriculture. Residents look at Prince George's today and see something more: hometown communities with good schools, churches, and stores, major league sports, and recreational facilities surrounded by plenty of wide open spaces. In short, they see a good place to raise a family.

It was Prince George's extensive wa-

terway network that first made the territory accessible to settlement and trade. Tribes of Indians were well established along the rivers by 1634, when Leonard Calvert, the second son of the first Lord Baltimore, sailed up the Potomac into Piscataway Creek in what is now the southwestern foot of the county. The colonists were received, although not enthusiastically, by the emperor Opechancanough. They decided to retreat downriver and establish Maryland's first colony where resident tribes were more hospitable. Finding the up-river soil ideal for the colony's expressed purpose of growing tobacco, though, settlers soon spread northward again, establishing manors on 1,000- and 2,000-acre grants fronting the navigable waterways.

By 1695 the Colonial population had grown to 1,700, and residents petitioned the governor and assembly to erect a separate county. Cut from Charles County, its neighbor to the south, the new jurisdiction was established on April 23, 1696—St. George's Day. It was named, however, for Prince George of Denmark, husband of Denmark's Queen Anne. As originally drawn, the county extended north as far as Pennsylvania and westward beyond the Blue Ridge Mountains as far as mapmakers had room to draw.

The new county also received an official seal bearing the arms of Queen Anne and a motto, *Semper Eadem: Ever the Same.* For more than a century the words seemed to contradict the stately but sure pace of the county's growth. A town "to be made after the Duke of Marlborough" was established in 1706; the county courthouse was moved to the town, duly named Upper Marlborough, 12 years later. (The name was later changed to its present spelling—Marlboro.) Lords of the manors built elegant estates whose Georgian style, patrician names and social organization echoed

the feudal sensibilities of seventeenth-century England. Many owners adorned their manors with autobiographical names, much like vanity license plates today: Beall's Pleasure, Brook's Reserve, His Ladyship's Highness, Darnall's Chance, and Cranford: His Adventure. By 1730 the population of the county was already nearing 10,000, mostly settled along the Patuxent River.

In 1746 the owners of the Belair manor, now part of Bowie, imported the Prince of Wales' prize stallion and a champion mare to establish the first thoroughbred horse racing stud farm in the New World. George Washington was one of the enthusiasts who wagered at the races at Upper Marlboro; although first in the hearts of his countrymen, he did not always bet on the horse that was always first over the finish line. A town built at Garrett's Landing above the Potomac on the Anacostia River was named Bladens Borough and soon became a busy deep-water tobacco port. By 1770 a school teaching Latin, Greek, and Hebrew had been established there.

Confederate General Jubal Early was unsuccessful in his attempt to free Confederate prisoners of war from the Union jail at Point Lookout in Prince George's County. From Cirker, *Dictionary of American Portraits*

Like the rest of the Potomac region, Prince George's was barely touched by the Revolution, although the disruption in trade affected tobacco farms and ports. In postwar decades, the tobacco-based economy began to give way to other crops cultivated on smaller tracts of land.

When the federal government arrived in Washington, D.C., the travails of Abigail Adams and other official visitors soon proved the need for a reliable, overland route northeast to the nation's population and commercial centers. By 1812 the route from Georgetown to Baltimore had been improved and was opened as a toll road just in time to let the British march in through Bladensburg to burn the capital in August 1814. Just two decades later the Baltimore and Ohio Railroad chugged into Washington along the same route; and in 1844

Samuel F.B. Morse spanned Prince George's County with the nation's first telecommunications system when he transmitted, "What hath God wrought" from the capital to Baltimore.

Like most of the region surrounding the capital, Prince George's County was presumed to be sympathetic to the South during the Civil War. Some local newspapers were surpressed by Union authorities; but except for an unsuccessful attempt by rebel raider Jubal Early to free Confederate prisoners of war from the Union jail at Point Lookout, no actual fighting took place on county soil. Four days after the war ended, however, the road to Clinton became infamous when John Wilkes Booth used it to escape the capital after he assassinated President Abraham Lincoln in Washington, D.C.

The war did hasten the end of many of the county's remaining tobacco-growing manors. Some evolved into smaller farms, where vegetables and livestock were raised without slave labor. Tracts near railway stations were sold to developers who turned them into subdivisions. By the turn of the century, more new developments grew as trolley lines from the District inspired a rush to the convenient eastern suburbs. Prince George's population, which had increased by only 20,000 in the 170 years since 1730, doubled from 30,000 to 60,000 between 1900 and 1930.

Cramped by the District's boundaries, a sprawling federal government increasingly took advantage of Prince George's cheap, plentiful, and, in contrast to the western suburbs, relatively flat land. The U.S. Army established its first pilot-training facility in 1909 at College Park; and in the 1930s the Department of Agriculture consolidated several government farm projects into the 8,000-acre Beltsville Agricultural Research Center. In 1939 the government designed the model town of Greenbelt to provide housing for lower-income federal employees, the precursor to many less attractive and much less successful housing projects that government agencies would build on the county's side of the District line in coming decades. In 1942 President Franklin Roosevelt established Andrews Air Force base, which later became home to the Strategic Air

Command. In the decade between 1930 and 1940, Prince George's population doubled to 120,000; by 1950 it was fast approaching 200,000.

As the federal government continued to expand during the 1960s, Prince George's was said to be the fastest-growing county in America. While Washington's upper-echelon executives moved up and out into the highland suburbs northwest of the city, the seemingly endless supply of inexpensive land in low-lying Prince George's attracted overflowing federal agencies and their more moderately paid workers. In 1961 the developer of the mass-market Levittown projects began a 9,000-home new town near Bowie on the grounds of Belair, the giant estate where thoroughbred horse breeding began in America more than 200 years before. Other large developments filled in the western crescent around the District of Columbia and extended out the northern arterial corridors. By 1969 the population stood at 640,000.

Ever improving roads, including the new Capital Beltway, put the county at the heart of an overland transportation network that included a passenger and freight rail's vital East Coast corridor. This network, adjacent to all that low-cost land, was desirable to manufacturers and distributors who made the county a primary warehouse center for regional shippers.

Recent decades have seen Prince George's leaders shift priorities from growth to more qualitative values. Efforts increased to attract private-sector companies that would provide local managerial and professional job opportunities to the county's growing work force. Planners also gained control of the county's rapid suburban sprawl by using sewer, water, and zoning powers to direct residential and commercial development. More subtle, but at least as important, county leadership instituted a

Goddard Space Flight Center attracts the nation's leading space scientists to Prince George's County. The facility is also a popular stop for tourists. Photo by Greg Pease

From its first campus in College Park, the University of Maryland has grown to a 12-campus, statewide system. Its flagship College Park campus alone serves more than 35,000 students. Photo by Walter Larrimore

campaign to change a widely held perception of Prince George's as the Potomac region's blue-collar stepchild. Significantly, the message was directed as much to the county's residents as to outsiders. Symbolizing the changing image, County Executive Winfield Kelly led a movement to scrap the longtime nickname, "P.G. County," which regional neighbors and the media then tended to use as a pejorative. Kelly would hear of nothing less than the county's full and regal title, Prince George's County.

All of those efforts have paid off. As Prince George's County approaches its fourth century, its citizens can take considerable pride not only in its big city neighbors but also in the resources within its own borders.

rose by at least one-third, and by 1991 almost 14,000 organizations, including prestigious names such as Digital Equipment, Litton Amecom, Maxima, Hechinger, Giant Food, Goddard Space Flight Center, and the International Association of Machinists employed about 250,000 workers there.

More than half of that increase was in the private sector, which now accounts for 78 percent of the jobs in the county, up from 65 percent a decade ago. Almost two-thirds of the new private-sector jobs were in the service, retail, and finance/insurance/real estate categories. As a result of all this business activity, the county's tax base more than doubled between 1980 and 1990, and median household effective buying in-

George Washington liked to watch the thoroughbreds race in Upper Marlboro's horse country; local gentry still celebrate the longstanding social traditions associated with the "sport of kings." Photo by Greg Pease

Facing page, bottom: John Carroll (1735-1815), the first bishop of the Roman Catholic Church in the United States, was born in Upper Marlboro. In 1789 Carroll established a Catholic college, which later became Georgetown University. Engraving by William Satchwell Leney and Benjamin Tanner, 1812, courtesy, National Portrait Gallery, Smithsonian Institution

To confirm its new attitude, in 1987 Prince George's was named an All-America City by the National League of Cities, the first county in five years to receive that honor. Long a crossroads, the county now offers a full choice of jobs, homes, schools, and parks in its own cities and towns. Once a waystation for the upwardly mobile, Prince George's has increasingly become a hometown where people move in to stay.

In recent years the county has been particularly successful in broadening and expanding its business community. During the 1980s at-place employment

come rose by 58 percent. As of 1988, Prince George's ranked 77th among 3,142 U.S. municipalities in per capita income.

Much of the business growth has been in high-technology service, manufacturing, and research and development industries. Such companies are drawn by Prince George's own long-standing and powerful high-tech core, particularly NASA's Goddard Space Flight Center and the University of Maryland.

Goddard, which was established in 1959, is a unique full-service facility that

can carry a project all the way from conceiving the mission and building the spacecraft to analyzing the data it transmits from the sky. Labs at Goddard are involved in many of NASA's high-profile projects, including the Hubble Telescope, Space Station Freedom, the Upper Atmosphere Research Satellite (UARS), and the Cosmic Background Explorer (COBE) satellite. Goddard's "spin-off" program works with business to transfer the technology developed in such projects to broader commercial applications. Goddard's National Space Science and Data Center is a massive clearinghouse for scientific information. The Center is also a leader in advanced data management and distribution technologies.

From its flagship campus at College Park, as well as from 11 other campuses throughout the state, the University of Maryland also shares its wealth of research and information. Systemwide, the university received more than $100 million in research contracts and grants in 1990 and aggressively pursues mutually productive ties with both the government and the private sector.

Much of the interaction is promoted by the university's interdisciplinary Engineering Research Center, which provides technical assistance and faculty expertise to business through its Technology Extension Service and develops business-oriented research through its Technology Initiatives Program. In its Technology Advancement Program, the Center has created a small business incubator, which provides space, facilities, and expertise for start-up companies producing high-tech products and services. Other programs promote cooperative research between school and business and summer internships for talented students.

Envisioning an even greater flow of skills and information, the University of Maryland is developing a Center for Science and Technology and a new 466-acre business campus near Bowie. The Supercomputing Research Center of the Institute for Defense Analyses is the first of a rarefied mix of tenants that will bring together university, industry, and government researchers in a collegial, creative atmosphere.

Other kinds of industries also find the resources they need in Prince George's County. One of Maryland's three Foreign Trade Zones is located within the 1,280-

Left: Naval officer Stephen Decatur (1779-1820), who was born in Sinepuxent, Maryland, served on the Board of Navy Commissioners, a post that eventually cost him his life. Captain James Barron, who accused Decatur of conspiring to block his promotion, challenged the commissioner to a duel. On March 22, 1820, Decatur was killed by Barron on the dueling ground near Bladensburg, Maryland. Painting by Gilbert Stuart. Courtesy, Independence National Historical Park. From Cirker, *Dictionary of American Portraits*

acre Collington Center south of Bowie; manufacturers there can receive, store, assemble, and transship foreign-made parts, bypassing customs.

Companies doing business in the international marketplace find that the University of Maryland's Center for International Business Education and Research at the College Park campus is another valuable neighbor. Funded by the U.S. Department of Education, the Center offers resources and support to U.S. companies marketing goods and services to Western and Eastern Europe, Asia, and Latin America. The University's East-West Science and Technology Center promotes high-tech informational exchanges and economic partnerships between U.S., and Eastern European producers.

Citizen efforts have preserved Victorian homes and mercantile buildings in the city of Laurel. Treasure hunters can find fine antiques and collectables at reasonable prices. Photo by Carol Highsmith Photography

For new businesses and future business owners, the Entrepreneurial Development Program at the historically black Bowie State University, now part of the University of Maryland system, offers a curriculum of management education, market information, and hands-on help. The Minority Business Opportunities Commission provides referral services and technical assistance to the county's numerous enterprises owned by blacks and members of other minority groups.

Business in Prince George's County can also count on a strong work force. In 1990 more than 420,000 of the county's 719,000 residents were actively in the labor market; of those, 47 percent worked within the county. To meet

training needs, employers can call on the Center for Business and Industry Training within the Prince George's Community College; likewise, the Investment in Job Opportunities program meets the growing need for entry-level workers by providing welfare recipients with training in basic job skills as well as daycare and other assistance so they can enter or reenter the job market.

The Prince George's Economic Development Corporation, a private corporation under contract to the county, prides itself on its ability to sever red tape for companies and developers. The EDC's innovative Priority Projects program encourages high-quality development by placing a short list of desirable new commercial and mixed-use projects on the fast track through the permits and approvals process. Their experts offer marketing assistance as well. Awarded on the basis of a project's design, feasibility, economic impact, minority participation, and other factors, "Priority" status is not conferred lightly. Forty-two projects earned it out of 12,000 building permits granted in 1990.

Partially as a result of the EDC's innovative efforts, office space in the county tripled between 1983 and 1990 to almost 24 million square feet. New commercial development includes the first phases of major mixed-use projects that will shape Prince George's skyline far into the future, including the Bowie New Town Center and the Rouse Company's Inglewood Business Community at Glenarden. Projects on the drawing board or just breaking ground foretell of the major urban center emerging at the crossroads of the Beltway, Route 50, Amtrak, and Metrorail in the Largo-Landover area. Others, such as the massive, visionary Port America on the banks of the Potomac, will soon edge major office and industrial employment centers along major highways well into the southern half of the county.

The presence of new business has enhanced, rather than overwhelmed, the hometown character that prevails in Prince George's County. It has enabled more Prince Georgians to work within an easy walk, drive, or Metro ride of where they live and has funded a tax base that has placed local schools, parks, and other services

among Maryland's best.

Community life is centered around the 28 separate cities and towns within the borders of the county. They offer a choice of life-styles. Populous, semiurban enclaves arc along the District line inside the Beltway. Peaceful country towns lie at rural crossroads farther south, where tobacco farmers still grow the famous Maryland Type 32-leaf along with other cash crops. Single-family homes nestle in suburban cul-de-sacs to the north and northeast. The numerous municipalities have encouraged citizens to remain close to local life and to cultivate each community's distinctive lore, institutions, and traditions. Unlike residents of many other suburban counties, Prince George' County Citizens have real places to call home.

Several of these towns are rooted in the county's earliest history, none more so than Upper Marlboro, the county seat. Settled in 1695 on the western branch of the Patuxent River and incorporated 11 years later, the town was a stop on the trade route between Port Tobacco to the south and the colonial capital at Annapolis and later became an official port of entry for the international tobacco trade. Site of the county court-

house since 1721, the town was a center of Colonial social and commercial life, home of a popular track for horse racing, and a stop for touring theatrical troupes.

Upper Marlboro's biggest fuss—and most repeated story—came about in 1814, when British soldiers made camp there before and after burning down Washington, D.C. Objecting to the soldiers' unseemly celebration, the local physician, Dr. William Beanes, had two of the rowdies jailed. Beanes was, in turn, arrested and hauled off to Baltimore with the British fleet. While on a British ship in Baltimore Harbor after negotiating Beanes' release, his lawyer, Francis Scott Key, watched Fort McHenry survive a night of bombardment and captured his thoughts in a poem titled "The Star Spangled Banner."

Except for some efficient-looking government buildings at its heart, Upper Marlboro remains a quiet, small town, as comfortable with the past as with the present. Markers explain the significance of local historic sites, including the 1735 birthplace of John Carroll, the first Catholic bishop in the United States, and his brother Daniel; the grave of Dr. William Beanes on the site of his home

Centuries-old trees frame Belair Mansion, the family home of three Maryland governors. The estate, built in 1746, also served as city hall for the City of Bowie. Photo by Ed Castle/Folio

near the schoolhouse pond; and the highway that was once a rolling road used by farmers to haul casks of tobacco to port. The red-brick Georgian house completed in the early 1700s by Henry Darnall on his manor, Darnall's Chance, has been restored as a county park and overlooks the town from a nearby hill.

Now part of the busy suburban core adjacent to the District of Columbia and the city of Hyattsville, Bladensburg was the scene of much coming and going for most of Prince George's County's history. An important seagoing port on the Anacostia River, Bladensburg was also on the overland road from Georgetown to Baltimore. During the early days of the nation, Bladensburg was the site of a notorious dueling ground, where two dozen men, including naval hero Stephen Decatur, were killed. The town was also the place where hastily assembled Americans attempted to halt British troops marching to invade the capital in 1814. Outgunned, the defenders quickly retreated, earning the battle its nickname, "the Bladensburg Races." For three years, between 1832 and 1835, the B & O Railroad terminated at Bladensburg because Congress refused to allow the line in the District. Despite the nearby development, several Colonial structures can be found in the old town.

At the county's northeastern edge, the city of Bowie stands on the site of a 1683 manor that later came to be known as Belair. In 1737 the estate was purchased jointly by the forebears of two of Maryland's most prominent families, the Ogles and the Taskers. It was Ogle who, in 1747, brought Spark, England's finest stallion, and Queen Mab, the top broodmare, to Belair and founded the New World's racing industry. A town grew up

around the Baltimore and Potomac Railroad line (which had come to the town in the 1870s), but it remained small until the Levitt Company developed its new town on the old Belair estate during the 1960s.

Bowie today is Prince George's third-largest municipality. With many of its original Victorian homes freshly restored, the city's historic core looks and feels like the ideal backdrop for a Fourth of July parade. Nearby the Levitt development has matured into a quiet, suburban town. The city is home to Bowie State University, part of the University of Maryland system, and just east is the University of Maryland's emerging Center for Science and Technology. The red-brick Georgian Belair Mansion belongs to the city, which is restoring it. Belair's grounds are graced by an avenue of tulip poplar trees, some of which were planted more than a decade before the Revolution. The Belair stables are now operated as a museum by the city.

Midway between Washington and Baltimore, the City of Laurel has prospered through the centuries because of its strategic position. Originally part of

the grand Montpelier estate, where Abigail Adams spent the night after getting lost on her way to the White House, the area saw increasing traffic and trade as the route grew into a turnpike, a stagecoach run, and, finally, the route of the B & O Railroad. In the nineteenth century the town was one of Prince George's few industrial areas, the home of large fabric mills powered by the Patuxent River. Later the town benefited as neighbor to Laurel Race Track and to Fort George G. Meade just across the border in Anne Arundel County. Today the city's historic preservation program has polished up many treasures on its streets and neighborhoods, including fine Victorian commercial architecture on Main Street, smartly painted and multi-gabled Queen Anne mansions, and the massive, masonry Avondale mill, where lace and tattings were produced until about 1900.

In coming decades Laurel stands to prosper even more as the keystone metropolitan area at Prince George's junction with Montgomery, Anne Arundel, and Howard counties. Major commercial and residential projects are planned and in progress both within Laurel and surrounding it in all four jurisdictions.

College Park and Berwyn Heights were all part of a 1745 manor known as Toaping Castle, named after the owner's former home in England. The Baltimore Road cut through these lands too, and, in 1798, the Rossborough Inn (still standing on the University of Maryland campus) was built and provided modest lodgings for cross-country travelers. When the railroad followed the turnpike, a town grew up around the station. After the Maryland Agricultural College was founded as a private enterprise in 1856, the town evolved into a pleasant Victorian academic community first called College Station and later College Park. The U.S. government established an airfield near College Park in 1909 so that Wilbur and Orville Wright could test their new flying machine for military use and train Army men to fly it. That airport remains the oldest in continuous use in the United States.

Just west, Berwyn Heights was one of several planned housing developments built during the 1880s along the railroad lines. Just south, the suburb of Riverdale grew on the site of the Riversdale estate,

Greenbelt's Scan Coop, which sells high-quality furniture and household items at competitive prices, is one of several innovative business and community ventures spawned in this "new town" developed in the 1930s. Photo by Greg Pease/Folio

owned by heirs of Lord Baltimore. Other Riversdale acreage became the Agricultural College.

Along with Takoma Park, which reaches into Montgomery County and the District, these communities flow together in a populous suburban corridor along the county's western edge, merging to the south with the city of Hyattsville. Hyattsville, named for its founder, Christopher Hyatt, developed from another 1880s railroad and trolley subdivision. A pleasant architectural blend of spacious, frame Victorian mansions, 1930s bungalows, postwar red-brick ramblers, and contemporary colonials, the city is an administrative hub for the growing north county region and home to Prince George's new Judicial Center.

Also part of the historic Toaping Castle grant, Greenbelt was the centerpiece in the federal government's New Deal efforts to create utopian planned communities with affordable housing. Inspired by the Garden City movement that originated in England, designer Rexford Tugwell clustered single and multifamily homes around amenities such as playgrounds and a community

shopping plaza and connected the clusters with parks, walkways, and natural areas. The town became a private cooperative, owned by its citizens in 1950. From the beginning Greenbelt attracted a special breed of suburban pioneers who were intrigued by its social philosophy. Many of today's community-minded residents work next door at Goddard Space Flight Center.

Thanks to strict architectural controls and continued care, the town's original core remains as a model of the era's visionary architecture and design, especially the art deco Greenbelt Center School, with its neoclassical relief facade sculpted by Work Progress Administration artist Lenore Thomas. At Greenbelt's edges, high-rise office buildings and hotels have established a busy high-tech and conference link with the university communities to the south. North of Greenbelt the National Agricultural Research Center is the focus of the unincorporated area Beltsville, which, in the early 1800s, was the Locust Grove Plantation owned by Truman Belt.

Just across the District line, the town of Fairmont Heights was home to many former slaves freed during and after the Civil War, while just west Seat Pleasant in Colonial times was the site of a church known as New Scotland. The church remained as a railroad town grew around it. Seat Pleasant, like its neighbors, Capitol Heights and District Heights, takes pride in being a pleasant community enclave in the midst of booming suburban development.

Also edging the District, Cheverly developed in the 1920s as a planned community on a former tobacco plantation named Mt. Hope. Today Cheverly remains a pleasant "island of green" in the busy suburban corridor. Just west the town of Glenarden is the historic hometown of many of the county's prominent black families and continues to be one of its most desirable residential suburbs. The new Inglewood business and conference center at Glenarden makes the area an increasingly important commercial community as well.

Inside the Beltway towns on arterial highways, such as North Brentwood and Brentwood, Mount Rainier, Cottage City, Edmonton, Landover Hills, Morningside, and Forest Heights have developed

The Enterprise Country Club and Golf Course plus miles of forested walkways and a swath of national parkland keep Greenbelt focused on the great outdoors. A "new town" of the 1930s, Greenbelt was inspired by England's Garden City movement. Photo by Greg Pease

in concert with growth in the District of Columbia. Many of the older communities are now experiencing growth and revitalization as new residents take advantage of their urban conveniences and suburban comforts. At the county's southern tip Eagle Harbor was incorporated with a population of two and remains a peaceful outpost on the Patuxent River.

Prince George's residential communities have continued to grow at a comfortable pace, even when the housing

From elementary through high school, magnet programs in Prince George's County public schools have become models for the nation. Efforts are helping substantially to close achievement gaps among county students. Photo by Pat Lanza Field/Folio

markets in nearby jurisdictions decline. The wealth of land enables builders to put reasonable price tags on even luxury homes; and the county's policy of "directed development" encourages new communities to be established only where the infrastructure is already in place to support them.

New residents migrating to Prince George's suburbs from the District of Columbia have accounted for much of the county's population increase in recent decades. The county has become the suburb of choice for the region's middle-class black families. As of the 1990 census, blacks now comprise 50.7 percent of its population, making the county one of the few predominately black suburbs in the nation. Increasingly, black residents have established strong social, cultural, and religious organizations in the county; and the county provides programs in history, arts,

and other interests to meet the needs of this growing population.

These efforts have been particularly successful in the public school system. Beginning the 1980s, Prince George's schools severely underfunded as the result of a tax rollback enacted by rebellious citizens, have bounced back with innovative programs praised as models for the nation. A magnet school system offers more than a dozen different specialized curricula, including science, French immersion, academics, biotechnology, humanities, international studies, and the performing arts at four dozen selected elementary, middle, and high schools. The system also offers magnet programs such as extended-day activities for elementary students and University High School for grades 9-12. Thanks to the magnet program, the system has achieved racial integration without bussing, while it continues to raise the students' level of achievement.

Some schools receive additional resources and staffing under the Milliken II program, which seeks to close achievement gaps among schools within the system. The Milliken II program, which provides for smaller classes and lower teacher-student ratios, full-time reading and library specialists, and additional teaching aids, including computers, has proved its worth. Students in the program now often outdo youngsters in other county public schools on standardized tests. Thanks to these and other programs, differences in overall test scores achieved by black and white students systemwide have been shrinking steadily since 1984.

Prince George's school system also takes pride in its more glossy symbols of achievement. One of these is the Challenger Center, where youngsters can work with the hardware of space exploration in a sophisticated hands-on array of computer and technical equipment. Prince George's was the only school system to be awarded a Challenger Center by a private foundation in honor of the space shuttle astronauts. County schools have also been visited by former President Ronald Reagan and First Lady Barbara Bush. In addition, teams from Eleanor Roosevelt High School in Greenbelt won the national "It's Academic" televised competition in 1988. In

1989 the county's graduating seniors earned $18.2 million in college scholarship money, an increase of more than 65 percent over the previous year.

Schools have been a focus of the county's aggressive drug prevention and education efforts, including Project DARE (Drug Abuse Resistance Education), which gives elementary school-children confidence and information to resist drug use. Increasingly, police officers are taking a community-oriented approach to crime prevention. New ACTION teams patrol neighborhoods on foot and work one-on-one with residents on neighborhood safety needs, while a midnight basketball league keeps vulnerable youngsters busy at hours when they might be tempted to become involved with drugs or other self-destructive behavior. Officers are trained in racial sensitivity and language skills so that they can work effectively with a county population that includes immigrants from more than 50 nations.

As Prince George's has matured, it has become ever more rich in the kinds of amenities that transform a suburb into a home. Within its borders are more than 16,000 acres of parkland, including four U.S. National Park Service preserves, and the Patuxent Wildlife Research Center, where endangered species raise their young peacefully on a protected 4,000-acre site just miles from urban centers. Some of the parks are allied with the county's 2,127 historic sites, such as the National Colonial Farm and Fort Washington, built in 1808 at a bend in the Potomac to guard the capital. Several colonial churches and mansions also remain in the county, including the Calvert family's own Riversdale. Other parks offer facilities for the kind of active recreation so popular with Prince George's families such as summer softball leagues, which field more than 600 teams on county playgrounds.

With the Capital Centre arena at Landover and the University of Maryland in College Park, Prince George's is a virtual lock as the capital of the region's major league sports as well. Capital Centre is the home of the Washington Bullets basketball team, which won the NBA championship in 1978; the Washington Capitals ice hockey team, which has evolved into a strong playoff contender

in the NHL; and a professional indoor lacrosse team. College Park's Maryland Terrapins athletic teams frequently achieve national rankings.

Such attractions now bring visitors from around the world to sample the pleasures of Prince George's County. They stroll through mansion grounds shaded by 200-year-old trees, spy a bald eagle's nest high in a tree in a wetland preserve, and cheer the Terrapins home on a crisp, football Sunday. Not surprisingly, they discover what Prince Georgians knew all along—that this crossroads county is also a most pleasant destination.

A national championship banner won by the Washington Bullets NBA basketball team hangs proudly in Capital Centre in Landover. The Capitals NHL hockey team also draws crowds to Capital Centre. Photo by Bert Goulait/*Washington Times*

Uniting the capital region with a swift, safe, and cost-effective rapid transit system, Metrorail is a cooperative effort by Congress, the District, and surrounding jurisdictions. Of the full, proposed 103-mile route, 89.5 miles are either complete or under construction. Photo by Neil Adams/Folio

. . . . .

Part Two

THE CAPITAL REGION'S ENTERPRISES

Chapter Six

NETWORKS

. . . .

Bridging the Gap

Maintaining a dynamic and consistent flow of power, people, and data, both inside and outside the capital region, is the responsibility of energy, transportation, and communication suppliers.

Photo by Matthew Borkoski/Folio

MEDIA GENERAL CABLE OF FAIRFAX

Above: Media General Cable of Fairfax has the distinction of serving more than 66 percent of Fairfax County's homes.

Right: Once a new customer initiates a connection request with the cable company, service technicians follow up immediately, often providing same-day service hookups.

Below: With its sophisticated information base, Media General Cable is able to transmit local news ranging from government to flight information.

With 97 channels of programming (and a system capacity of 120 channels), Media General Cable of Fairfax offers its subscribers the widest choice available in the industry.

"We want our customers to see cable television as a necessity, not as a luxury," says Thomas E. Waldrop, chairman and chief executive officer of Media General Cable of Fairfax. More than 198,000 Fairfax County homes already share that perception. The Media General Fairfax Cable system serves more than 66 percent of the county's homes, an urban-area penetration rate that is among the highest in the nation.

The cable company's success reflects the long-term commitment that Media General made when it first won the Fairfax County franchise. The system's parent company has invested more than $320 million in Fairfax County.

From the beginning, the company recognized that it was dealing with a uniquely knowledgeable and demanding audience. To meet the anticipated demands of that market, Media General set out to provide county residents with the latest cable system technology and the highest standards of customer service.

"Cable television is a customer-driven business," says Waldrop. "We know that our Fairfax County customers expect us to provide state-of-the-art technology and customer service."

The customer service system starts with one-stop shopping. New customers can initiate a connection request with a single telephone call. Service technicians follow up immediately, often providing same-day service hookups.

Fairfax County residents increasingly rely on the growing menu of local services. The system provides local news on Newschannel 8; several local government channels (Fairfax City, Herndon, and Falls Church); two Fairfax County public school channels; two college course channels; public access programming; and a library channel. For travelers, it provides regional traffic information, national weather, and flight information from both Dulles and National airports.

Waldrop extends his company's involvement in community service to include his personal life. He is a director of Fairfax Symphony and the Fairfax County Council of the Arts, and a member of the Regional United Way Council. He is also a member of the Fairfax County Schools' Business Advisory group.

A subsidiary of Media General Cable of Fairfax, Mega Advertising, manages the system's photo-classified advertising services. Mega also handles advertising sales for cable systems throughout the metropolitan Washington area, a combined subscriber base totaling nearly 500,000 cable homes.

Media General is a diversified communications company with major interests in newspapers, broadcasting, cable television, newsprint production, commercial printing, and publications. The company is headquartered in Richmond. J. Stewart Bryan III is chairman, president, and chief executive officer of Media General, Inc.

WKYS RADIO 93.9 FM

W̶KYS-FM is co-located at 4001 Nebraska Avenue in prestigious Northwest Washington with WRC-TV 4 and NBC-TV Network.

Prior to its acquisition by Albimar Communications Inc. in late 1988, the entire offices, studios, and technical facilities of WKYS-FM were re-equipped with state-of-the-art technology through a $3.1-million capitalized improvement plan.

WKYS-FM is one of the few market stations to play the majority of its musical product from CD. Significant investments were made in WKYS-FM's audio processing chain to provide unparalleled brightness, bass response, and high end capability.

In November 1989, WKYS-FM increased its antenna height, providing significant coverage between Richmond, Virginia, and Baltimore, Maryland.

WKYS-FM is the only Washington radio station able to offer off-site distribution (via microwave) from remote locations and have its own two-way radio system.

WKYS-FM is Washington's choice with a better selection of music. A wide variety of music is one of many reasons why the station is so appealing to the largest share of 25-54-year-old adults.

WKYS-FM has long been one of the capital's major radio stations. The urban-based music combined with news, public affairs, and information is why WKYS-FM remains the station of widest appeal to a diverse adult audience.

WKYS-FM programming leads the way with the talents of program director Barbara Prieto and the genius of nationally known celebrity Donnie Simpson, vice president of programming.

Through its unique mixture of rhythm & blues, hits, oldies, and jazz, WKYS-FM has created an elegant sound that its listeners

have come to associate with the station.

The news department regularly airs the issues affecting the Washington metropolitan area, providing thought-provoking and objective information. WKYS-FM's music-based product is supported by a professional staff who prepare and distribute 55 live newscasts weekly. It is one of a few D.C. stations to be computerized using the Associated Press. Fifteen daily reports are provided by "Metro Traffic."

WKYS-FM believes in servicing the interests and needs of its community. Each year the station surveys 225 community leaders to solicit the information necessary to develop programs that meet the community's needs.

In addition, the news, public affairs, and programming departments regularly produce shows that address topical issues of relevance and importance to the audience.

WKYS-FM creative services department coordinates sponsorship packages for some of Washington's largest events with the sales, programming, and public affairs teams to help raise hundreds of dollars for various charities and, at the same time, entertain its listeners.

Marketing at WKYS-FM means promoting clients' products and brands to the WKYS-FM audience. Every year WKYS-FM appears live and in person to more than 1.5 million family-oriented listeners.

Above: The WKYS-FM morning team. From left to right are Tony Perkins, Donnie Simpson, and John Irving.

Below: WKYS-FM's news department regularly produces shows that address topical issues of importance to the station's audience.

Television's "The MacNeil-Lehrer Newshour" and "Washington Week in Review," and radio's "Millennium of Music," have made the WETA stations a vital part of the American cultural atmosphere. These regularly scheduled programs and such special broadcasts as "A Capital Fourth" are carried by public broadcasting stations across the nation. All are produced locally by Washington's own WETA Television 26 and WETA Radio FM91.

WETA Television 26 is also the producer of Ken Burns' remarkable television series, "The Civil War," and also "Empire of the Air," a history of radio.

WETA Channel 26 and WETA Radio FM91 are noncommercial, member-supported public broadcasting stations. They provide the greater Washington community with a culturally enriched menu of commercial-free entertainment, public affairs and informational programming, and educational television.

Approximately 1.85 million viewers tune in to WETA Television 26 programs each week. Another 339,000 Washington area residents are regular listeners to WETA Radio FM91.

Production costs, program acquisition, broadcasting activities, and other operating expenses of the WETA stations are financed by member contributions and by corporate underwriting.

Members provide more than 60 percent of the funding for local radio operations. Corporations and foundations provide funding to support or underwrite the balance of WETA activities. For example, the General Motors Corporation provided much of the funding required for production of "The Civil War."

WETA Television 26 provides the Washington community with a wide range of popular shows provided through the Public Broadcasting Service network. They include "Sesame Street" and other children's programs, such adult entertainment favorites as "Masterpiece Theatre" and "Mystery!," news

and public affairs programs such as "Firing Line" and "Wall Street Week," and many others.

WETA Television 26 also produces and broadcasts programs for and about the Washington community such as "Around Town," Washington's only weekly revue of the arts on television, "Metro Week," a local-interest version of the nationally broadcast "Washington Week in Review."

WETA Radio FM91 follows a classical music programming format. Its news and information programs include "All Things Considered" (produced by National Public Radio), "MonitoRadio," and "Marketplace." Most of the station's musical programming is locally produced, including "Music from Washington," which features performances recorded live at locations throughout the city.

Nationally broadcast programs produced

by WETA Radio FM91 include WETA's broadcasts of Baltimore Symphony Orchestra concerts; "Folk Masters," a program of traditional music recorded at New York's Carnegie Hall; and "Millennium of Music," which was broadcast locally in Washington for 12 years before becoming a national program in 1991.

The WETA stations are located in the Shirlington Gateway neighborhood of Arlington county. WETA was founded in 1961 by Elizabeth Campbell. Sharon Percy Rockefeller is president and chief executive officer.

Above: Robert MacNeil and Jim Lehrer co-anchor "The MacNeil/Lehrer NewsHour," television's only one-hour national nightly news program.
Photo by Chris Little

Right: Elmo, a favorite character on "Sesame Street." WETA TV 26 devotes more than one-third of its program hours to children.
Photo courtesy of Childrens Television Workshop.

THE WASHINGTON TIMES

In September 1991, with the national economy (and advertising revenues) still "recessed," *The Washington Times* added Saturday and Sunday editions to its traditional, Monday - Friday publishing schedule. To many, it seemed a clear case of swimming against the stream. Times staffers happily agreed.

The Washington Times has been bucking the trendy Washington establishment since the paper was launched in May 1982.

"The pretensions of Washington newspapermen, particularly those who think of themselves as 'journalistic entities,' have always amused me," says Wesley Pruden, managing editor of *The Washington Times*. Pruden joined the paper as chief political correspondent just three months after the paper began publication. He spent his first day on the job in Beirut.

"We take our jobs seriously at *The Times*," says Pruden, "but God help us from ever taking ourselves seriously."

With a circulation hovering around the 100,000 mark, *The Times* does daily combat with the comfortably established *Washington Post*. "Real journalism is war," says Pruden, "and you can't fight a war on white wine and Perrier."

The Washington Times fights with splashy graphics and timely news coverage. The paper even published "EXTRA!" editions when Washington Mayor Marion Barry was arrested on cocaine possession charges, and when a "mistrial" got him off on most of them. It published another "EXTRA!" at the start of the war in the Persian Gulf. The special editions won nationwide attention for the newspaper and the Society of Newspaper Design's Gold Award.

The Washington Times has also won industry recognition (and advertiser support) for its special sections: "Auto Weekend" in Friday issues of the paper, and "Today's Home," published on Thursdays.

"Today's Home" section responds directly to the life-style requirements of *Washington Times* readers," says Michael Mahr, director of advertising. "The Auto Weekend section has become the number one automotive section in the Washington area."

That fits perfectly with the "hometown newspaper" ethic of *The Washington Times*. The paper has played close attention to local events, issues, and leaders. But no journalist can ignore the fact that some very powerful people call Washington home. *The Times* has become an influential voice. President Ronald Reagan made it clear that *The Times* was his preferred source of news.

The Washington Times is owned and published by The Washington Times Corporation, a wholly owned subsidiary of News World Communications, Inc. Bo Hi Pak is chairman and president of The Washington Times Corporation. Ronald S. Godwin is senior vice president.

"Despite the proliferating media in today's world, it's not always easy to find the information you really need," says Godwin. Godwin describes his company's target audience as "people who continue to search for publications that better inform and communicate." One of the hallmarks of The Washington Times Corporation, says Ranzer, "is innovation. We have to be better to compete successfully."

Another hallmark of *The Washington Times* is that it always seems to buck the trend, fly in the face of "politically correct" establishment thinking, and survive to tell the tale.

Above: Managing Editor Wesley Pruden takes a final look at a proof of *The Washington Times'* "extra" edition devoted to coverage of the beginning of the Persian Gulf war.

Left: The Washington Times' headquarters at 3600 New York Avenue, N.E. in Washington, D.C.

THE JOURNAL NEWSPAPERS

Above: The Springfield, Virginia, printing facility for the Journal Newspapers.

Right: The Goss Colorliner at the Journal printing plant is capable of printing newspapers with an unlimited number of high-quality 4-color pages.

The Journal Newspapers, headquartered in Fairfax, Virginia, publishes five daily and 10 weekly newspapers, serving the suburban communities of Montgomery and Prince Georges counties in Maryland and the Northern Virginia jurisdictions of the city of Alexandria and Fairfax, Arlington, and Prince William counties.

The Journals began as a response to the unprecedented growth taking place during the early 1970s in the suburban communities surrounding the District of Columbia.

Editorially, the time was ripe for a newspaper that would reflect and speak to the information needs that made suburban families so different from those in the city. And from a marketing standpoint, such a vehicle would provide a selective advertising medium for retailers to reach and sell to those big-spending families.

In December 1971 the company purchased *The Alexandria Journal*, a small weekly with about 2,000 paid subscribers. During the next four years, that single newspaper was joined by *The Arlington Journal* and *The Fairfax Journal* in Virginia and by *The Montgomery Journal* and *The Prince George's Journal* in suburban Maryland. Together, they formed a ring of editorial and advertising coverage around the nation's capital.

By 1977 The Journal Newspapers had expanded from weekly to twice-weekly frequency. And in 1981 the demise of the daily *Washington Star* prompted The Journals to expand to become suburban Washington's daily, Monday-through-Friday newspapers.

In the latter part of the 1980s, the company moved to broaden its household penetration throughout the suburbs. Weekly Journals were introduced in Montgomery, Prince George's, and Fairfax counties as well as in Prince William County, the newest frontier in Northern Virginia's expanding suburbs. The weeklies are mailed free to single-family households that do not subscribe to one of the dailies.

Today, The Journal Newspaper Network has become a highly respected member of the suburban Washington community. For more than 570,000 area households, The Journals fill the local information void left by the world and national focus of the metropolitan dailies and area broadcast media. As these communities have grown and prospered, their residents have increasingly turned to The Journal. In December, 1991, Newsco, Inc. acquired The Journal Newspapers.

The Journal Newspapers have successfully established the proper niche for themselves in this very desirable market.

The Journals represent an important opportunity for businesses of all sizes and types. Advertisers can efficiently target their marketing message to a very select segment of the suburban Washington market. Or they may gain broad market-wide exposure throughout the suburbs by using the full network.

In terms of home ownership, household income, investment patterns, leisure activities, and spending habits, Journal readers are the most active and attractive consumers that this market has to offer.

Advertisers know that because of the quality of these newspapers and the interests and life-style of their readers, The Journals enjoy a loyal, thorough attention from the suburban population they serve.

Photo by Robert Llewellyn

Chapter Seven

BUSINESS AND PROFESSIONS

■ ■

A Flourishing Mecca of Opportunity

The capital region's business and professional community brings a wealth of service, ability, and insight to the area.

Photo by Greg Pease

NATIONAL COOPERATIVE BANK

Above: NCB's new headquarters at The Franklin Tower, located at 14th and Eye streets, NW.

Right: Greenbelt Homes, located in Greenbelt, Maryland, enjoys a national reputation as one of the largest and most successful self-managed and diversified housing cooperatives.

When a group of working parents in Arlington County, Virginia, wanted to start a day care center, they came face to face with harsh financial reality. Traditional banks thought the venture too risky and its future too unpredictable. A local real estate developer provided a location, but without credit, there was no way to purchase furniture or hire teachers. Without teachers, they could not recruit children.

The solution came from a bank that few of the parents even knew existed: National Cooperative Bank. NCB evaluated the business plan, looked over the site, and provided start-up financing. Today the center serves 75 families. For the parents who started the cooperative, the financing was a miracle. For NCB, it was business as usual.

NCB helps businesses created by people who work together to help themselves. As an organization created to support the cooperative movement, NCB promotes voluntarism, cooperation, and economic self-reliance. It helps cooperative organizations achieve self-sufficiency, not by giving them a handout, but through responsible, and occasionally nontraditional, banking.

There is much more to this organization than theory. NCB is in business to serve, on a mutually profitable basis, the growing financial requirements of cooperative businesses. NCB itself is an outstanding example of the kinds of achievement made possible by skill-

ful application of cooperative principles. At year-end 1991, NCB's assets totaled more than $500 million.

Headquartered in Washington, NCB is a customer-owned organization that promotes and finances cooperatively structured businesses and organizations nationwide. It also provides cooperatives with information on where to obtain technical advice and related assistance. It has offices in New York, Minneapolis, Seattle, and Anchorage. In 1990 NCB expanded its presence in Atlanta, Chicago, Austin, and San Francisco.

NCB does not accept deposits from the general public. Rather, it is a diversified financial services company providing mortgage banking, commercial lending, access to capital markets, and commercial depository services. It is the only American bank created exclusively to provide financial services to all sectors of the cooperative marketplace.

Cooperatives are businesses owned and controlled by their employees, their customers, or the people they serve. Once con-

sidered "visionary" or even "radical" experiments, successful cooperatives now operate throughout the American economy and throughout the world.

Recreational Equipment, Inc. (REI) is America's largest and best-known consumer co-op. Other industries with active cooperative components include child care, health care, retailer-owned wholesale, rural electrification, and many agricultural processing and marketing groups.

In the increasingly popular area of Employee Stock Ownership Plans, NCB has become a leading advocate and financier.

NCB comprises a group of related corporations. NCB Development Corporation lends start-up funds for higher-risk and low-income cooperatives. It works directly with housing developers, community development corporations, and local housing authorities to assist with start-up cooperatives.

NCB Mortgage Corporation services loans originated by NCB or third-party lenders. Such loans may be purchased or sold in secondary mortgage markets. In 1990 *American Banker* ranked NCBMC as 190 on the list of America's top 300 mortgage companies.

Cooperative Funding Corporation specializes in corporate finance. It arranges financing, on a fee-for-service basis, on behalf of cooperatives that may not be able to access the capital markets directly. NCB Business Credit Corporation makes asset-based, collateralized loans and leases to cooperatively structured businesses.

NCB Capital Corporation secures capital worldwide to position NCB as a reliable source of financing for cooperatives. NCB Financial Corporation is a holding company, formed primarily to hold the stock of NCB Savings Bank, FSB, located in Ohio.

NCB was created under the terms of the National Consumer Cooperative Bank Act of 1978. Passage of the act marked the successful culmination of three years of legislative efforts by a broad coalition of urban and rural consumer cooperatives and community-based organizations. In 1981 NCB became the first government corporation to be fully privatized. A unique arrangement made possible a leveraged buy-out that moved NCB from the public to the private sector where the customers of the bank became its owners. Financing for the buy-out came from the U.S. Treasury. The bank agreed to repay the treasury over a 40-year period.

NCB became fully operational in 1980. From the beginning, it followed conservative policies. Innate prudence and adherence to the cooperative philosophy of user ownership helped NCB avoid heavy investment in junk bonds and real estate speculation. As a result, the bank has continued to expand and to increase its profitability.

In 1989 both Standard and Poor's Corporation and Duff and Phelps, Inc., recognized NCB's stability, assigning their highly favorable "investment grade" ratings to NCB's securities. By 1990 NCB had fulfilled its creators' hopes and expectations. It had become a broad based institution capable of meeting most of the financial needs of consumer cooperatives throughout the country.

"Cooperatives are the most fundamental form of capitalism," says Charles E. Snyder, president and chief executive officer of NCB. "They enhance competition, build markets, reduce costs to the consumer, keep businesses alive, and spread capitalism by transforming employees into owners.

"For all this to happen there has to be a fi-

nancial institution that understands the very structure of cooperation among businesses and individuals. Everywhere, new ventures are being formed based on the strengths of cooperation and the recognition that in the next century both the opportunities and challenges to America will be enormous. Cooperation pools the strengths of many different interests, while retaining individual interests. It is likely that the cooperative philosophy of this century will dominate business thinking of the next."

Above: Pictured here is one of the more than 8,000 True Value stores and a member of Cotter and Company, the largest cooperative hardware wholesaler in the United States.

Left: GHA, founded in 1937, is one of the largest managed health care companies in the Washington area.

THOMAS HAVEY & COMPANY

"The Big-8 is now the Big-6," says Bill Voorhees, managing partner of Thomas Havey & Co.'s Washington, D.C., office, "and there is no doubt that the business landscape for our profession has undergone significant change. But, we find our company in the middle of an exciting and expanding practice." Voorhees, along with his five Washington partners, believes the 44-year-old company occupies a strong position to serve Washington-area organizations with personalized and resource-backed services.

Founded in 1948, the firm of Thomas Havey & Co. has built its full-service certified public accounting practice on a foundation of commitment to personal service. Operating out of Chicago, Minneapolis, Baltimore, and Philadelphia—in addition to the Washington office—the firm is one of a shrinking handful

Partner Steven Raeder, managing partner William Voorhees, and partner Melvin Harris are all longtime Washington natives.

of large- to medium-sized accounting firms remaining independent of the profession's international giants. "We're the right size to offer the best of both worlds," says Voorhees, indicating the strength of number (250 employees nationwide, 80 in Washington) and the breadth of consistent expertise and longevity among the professional staff.

"In Washington," says Stephen Raeder, another Thomas Havey & Co. partner whose native ties to the Washington area include substantial civic involvement with a number of members from the educational, social, and religious communities, "our clients are accustomed to picking up the phone and talking to the individual with the most appropriate knowledge to solve their problems; be that a partner or a member of our

professional accounting, tax, or consulting staffs."

To ensure this depth of expertise, Thomas Havey & Co. returns a significant percentage of its earnings back to its people in the form of training and professional certification. Says Raeder, "we want our clients to know that they can get their questions answered professionally and promptly."

And, with this basic philosophy, many Washington organizations since 1979 have chosen Thomas Havey & Co. as their accounting firm, resulting in a positive and steady growth for the firm. Melvin Harris, the firm's technical partner and another longtime Washington-area resident, recalls that when Thomas Havey & Co. merged with his prior firm, McGinley, Roche and Mallory, the practice "continued to reflect and expand upon what we had established here for our Washington clients since the late 1930s; a commitment to offering superior, personal service to a diverse range of commercial and not-for-profit organizations."

Now overlooking historic Farragut Square from the corner of Seventeenth and I streets, Thomas Havey & Co. is within walking distance or a short Metro ride of many of its clients. These include representatives of the Washington university, membership association, and political and advocacy group communities so prevalent in the District of Columbia and its surrounding metropolitan areas. The firm is also a recognized leader in accounting and consulting to multi-employer pension and welfare funds, and on the commercial side, it has developed a growing practice serving real-estate and property management enterprises.

"We see the firm continuing to build our practice and broaden our areas of knowledge," says Voorhees. "But in doing so, never losing sight of what has brought us the loyalty of our clients—being there for them when they need us."

JONES, DAY, REAVIS & POGUE

The Litigation Center in the Jones Day Washington office. Photo by Bill Pappas

Founded in Cleveland, Ohio, in 1893, Jones, Day, Reavis & Pogue is now one of the largest law firms in the country and ranks second in size in the world. The firm's 20 offices are strategically located throughout the United States, Europe, Asia, and the Middle East.

Jones Day includes approximately 1,200 attorneys worldwide. The firm's Washington, D.C., office, with more than 200 lawyers, is one of Jones Day's largest and most active offices.

The Washington office, which houses one of the firm's state-of-the-art Litigation Centers, is located at 1450 G Street, N.W. Jones Day's practice focuses on five major areas: corporate, government regulation, litigation, real estate, and tax law. Its clients include approximately half of the top *Fortune* 500 corporations.

Jones Day lawyers are supported by advanced technology systems that provide the most complete information possible. Attorneys are linked via a sophisticated computer network to clients, other Jones Day attorneys and offices, and external information retrieval systems. The firm also has video capabilities designed to assist attorneys in associate and expert witness training. The electronic system is backed up by one of the nation's largest private legal libraries.

The technological assets of Jones Day not only serve clients' needs, but also attract top-notch legal talent to the firm.

Approximately 153 of its lawyers held prestigious judicial clerkships upon law school completion and 19 served as clerks to justices of the U.S. Supreme Court. Jones Day includes numerous distinguished former public servants, and many of the firm's former members currently hold important positions of public trust.

The key to Jones Day's unique practice is that it operates its global network as a single, unified law firm. Attorneys join the firm knowing that they are joining a national and international practice, one that may call upon them to provide assistance anywhere that their particular expertise is required.

The ability to respond quickly and effectively, regardless of geographic location, has been a factor in the selection of Jones Day as litigation counsel by major national and international companies. The firm has four Litigation Centers strategically located across the country, including the one in Washington. Each Litigation Center functions as a self-contained support facility.

Jones Day opened its Washington office in 1946, making the firm one of the first non-Washington-based law firms to establish an office in that city. Today many members of the Washington office participate in civic and community affairs, and several are leaders of global philanthropic organizations, demonstrating that Jones Day lawyers are committed to giving back to the community in which they are located and from which they receive so much.

CRESTAR BANK

Crestar Financial Corporation is a strong regional institution where customer service is the top priority. Crestar customers have come to expect innovative and attractive financial alternatives to meet both their business and personal needs.

Crestar Financial Corporation is the holding company for Crestar Bank N.A. of Washington, D.C., Crestar Bank MD of Maryland, and Crestar Bank of Virginia. Crestar and its predecessor banks have been serving the national capital region since the early 1800s. These roots provide Crestar with a unique blend of strengths in both commercial and consumer banking.

Crestar remains committed to the local marketplace. It provides a full range of competitive financial programs. By consolidating operations, sustaining a strong financial position, and maintaining the highest standards for quality customer service, Crestar has won the loyalty of clients and the respect of competitors throughout the region.

One of the exciting developments at Crestar is the construction of a state-of-the-art lockbox facility, located in Columbia, Maryland. Another is the establishment of a not-for-profit division

with highly skilled employees trained to serve the specific financial needs of nonprofit organizations.

Other developments include an expansion of the private banking group to better serve its clients, and advanced, specialized training for employees. Crestar employees are uniquely equipped to handle the detailed processing required by government contract work and similar highly specialized tasks.

With nearly 6,000 employees, Crestar operates 265 banking offices and 233 automated teller machines (ATMs). This includes 101 offices and 105 ATMs in the greater Washington metropolitan area. Four subsidiaries provide mortgage, insurance, security, and investment advisory services. As of June 30, 1992, Crestar held $11.5 billion in total assets and $9.5 billion in total deposits.

Crestar's growth in recent years has been dramatic, particularly in the Washington area. The acquisition of Perpetual Savings Bank added 22 new offices and substantial deposits. In all, Crestar has acquired 11 financial institutions over the past five years.

"As a service organization and a corporation that owes much of its success to the people and businesses in our local markets, Crestar is committed to being an active, working partner in the communities in which we serve," says William C. Harris, president of Crestar's greater Washington region.

This partnership is reflected in Crestar's financial commitment to purchasing bond funds through the D.C. Housing Finance Agency, and financial assistance to many organizations such as Development Corporation of Columbia Heights, Neighborhood Housing Development Corporation, and the Washington Urban League.

Many individual Crestar employees volunteer their time, talent, and leadership skills, serving on local task forces, committees, and boards of directors. This list is long and distinguished and includes the National Symphony, the Fairfax Chamber of Commerce, the Federal City City Council, and The Greater Washington Board of Trade.

MCGUIRE, WOODS, BATTLE & BOOTHE

Since its nineteenth century beginnings, McGuire, Woods, Battle & Boothe has expanded through mergers and a growing client base into one of America's 60 largest law firms. With more than 340 lawyers practicing in five offices across Virginia, as well as in Baltimore, Maryland, the District of Columbia, Brussels, Belgium, and Zurich, Switzerland, its work includes all aspects of civil practice in local, state, national, and international jurisdictions. Their offices are positioned in the heart of the mid-Atlantic region within the "Golden Crescent" running from Norfolk through Richmond, Northern Virginia, and Washington to Baltimore. About one-half of the nation's population lives within a 500-mile radius. The Brussels office anchors the transatlantic clients they serve throughout Europe and the rest of the globe.

In the process of this expansion "we stayed diversified and that gives us general appeal— to businesses seeking specialized expertise and depth in litigation or corporate representation, to clients who need help with tax planning or a real estate transaction, and to individuals who need reliable counsel for personal matters," says Dennis McArver, managing partner of the firm's Tysons Corner office.

The Tysons Corner office is a mainstay in regional real estate and land use matters. McGuire, Woods represented Robert E. Simon when he first conceived the "new town" of Reston, and has represented that planned community's developers since then. It currently represents the giant office park near Dulles Airport, Westfields. When completed, Westfields will be the largest single commercial development in the Washington metropolitan area.

Alexandria is the home of the U.S. District Court for the Eastern District of Virginia. Appropriately, the Alexandria office concerns itself primarily with litigation. The firm's Washington, D.C., office involves itself primarily with the U.S. Congress and various federal agencies. The practice is especially active in securities law, labor law, international law, environmental affairs, transportation, and other administrative and regulatory issues. The firm's Baltimore office enjoys a general civil practice with emphasis on energy, tax, banking, corporate, and real estate matters.

Other major clients of the firm include

Above: The Washington, D.C., office of McGuire, Woods, Battle & Boothe. Photo by Lautman Photography

Left: Tysons Corner Office. Photo by Lautman Photography

some of the largest banks in the Commonwealth, James River Corporation, CSX, Crown Central Petroleum, several local government agencies and entities, high technology corporations, and hospitals. "The combination of our expertise in specialties and our expansive knowledge of the more traditional generalized practice of law has positioned us to be of particular value to corporations relocating to the Washington metropolitan area," says McArver. "We have close, mutually respectful relationships with state, county, and city governments. We have outstanding experience and expertise in all aspects of business law as well as litigation experience that only comes after more than a century of practicing law in a vital, complex business climate."

FREDDIE MAC

Right: Leland Brendsel, chairman and chief executive officer. Photo by Bill Denison

Below: Freddie Mac is dedicated to making the American dream of decent, accesible housing a reality.

Freddie Mac (the Federal Home Loan Mortgage Corporation) is a stockholder-owned corporation. It was chartered by Congress in 1970 to create a continuous flow of funds to mortgage lenders in support of home ownership and of rental housing.

Freddie Mac plays an important role in pumping funds into mortgages for low- and moderately-priced housing. The average single-family loan purchased by Freddie Mac in recent years has been well under $100,000. One-fourth of new loans purchased by the corporation are for less than $75,000.

In the rental market, Freddie Mac purchases mortgages on multifamily buildings. Many units typically provide housing for low- and moderate-income families.

Freddie Mac accomplishes its goals by linking the capital markets with the home buyer or apartment building owner. By making money for housing available to all areas of the country, Freddie Mac has stabilized the availability of mortgage funds and helped to lower rates to borrowers. By creating a nationwide mortgage market, Freddie Mac has provided lenders in depressed and prosperous regions with equal access to capital.

In the process, Freddie Mac has established its new McLean, Virginia, headquarters as a major American financial marketplace. Billions of dollars flow through its operations daily.

In building its success, Freddie Mac has made itself an international center of mort-

gage finance expertise and created an entire new class of attractive investment instruments. The secondary mortgage market has continued to increase the national availability of mortgage financing, despite recent widespread disruptions in the thrift industry.

Actually, the uncertainties associated with other investment opportunities have increased the attractiveness of Freddie Mac's securities. "The capital market's search for high-quality instruments has brought increasing investment to Freddie Mac," explains Leland C. Brendsel, chairman and chief executive officer of Freddie Mac. "That, in turn, has increased the capital available to the mortgage market throughout America."

Freddie Mac operates by purchasing mortgage loans originated by banks, savings and loan institutions, mortgage bankers, and other lenders throughout the nation. It repackages those loans as Freddie Mac securities for sale to investors.

Freddie Mac securities are not guaranteed by the federal government. They are backed, instead, by the corporation's financial strength and reputation. To protect the quality of its securities, Freddie Mac relies on several proven business strategies. It guarantees geographical diversity by purchasing loans throughout the United States, maintains high underwriting criteria, works only with qualified primary lenders, and rigorously employs several other layers of protection and management oversight.

As a result, Freddie Mac securities are highly regarded throughout the world. Investors include financial institutions, pension funds, insurance companies, and foreign investors.

Freddie Mac instruments are attractive securities that provide investors with regular payments based on the amounts paid by the actual borrowers each month. As a result, the

investor is able to enjoy the competitive returns, regular income, and security of residential mortgage investments.

During its first 20 years of operation, Freddie Mac has sold more than $500 billion in mortgage-backed securities.

Freddie Mac uses the income from the sale of securities to purchase additional mortgages loans. The existence of this secondary market for mortgages allows banks and other direct lenders to make more money available to home purchasers on a continual basis.

"Home ownership is an enduring national

"Another way we're addressing America's housing needs is working with state and local governments and concerned private-sector firms," says Glenn. "We look for partners to share in the down payment as it is typically the biggest hurdle for the first-time home buyer to overcome."

Philanthropically, Freddie Mac actively supports programs working with disadvantaged youth. "Reach Out to a Child" is a corporate activity to raise the national awareness of neglected and abandoned children. "Reach Out to a Child" works to en-

An exterior view of Freddie Mac headquarters in McLean, Virginia.

priority," says Brendsel. "Aiding those striving to achieve the American dream is high on the national agenda, and on Freddie Mac's agenda. We accept as part of our mission the responsibility to aid affordability by attracting private dollars to the public priority of housing."

To directly assist people who want to purchase single-family homes, Freddie Mac participates in special pilot programs designed to lower home buyers' down payments. Under these programs, purchasers may devote a higher than average percentage of their monthly income to housing. Through community groups, borrowers receive home-buyer education and counseling assistance.

"The important thing," says Freddie Mac president and chief operating officer David W. Glenn, "is that the project makes sense financially. We look for community involvement through a local mortgage insurer or a local partnership that will help share the risk.

courage foster care, adoption, and family preservation. Among other activities, it sponsors seminars operated through the Washington Metropolitan Area Council of Governments.

In addition to its international headquarters in McLean, Freddie Mac operates four regional offices: Arlington, Virginia (Northeast); Chicago, Illinois (North Central); Atlanta, Georgia (Southeast/Southwest); and Sherman Oaks, California (Western).

Freddie Mac common stock is traded on the New York Stock Exchange. In mid-1992 corporate assets totaled well over $50 billion. To date, the company has helped to finance one of every eight homes in America.

By continuing to build investor confidence, Freddie Mac will continue to address the affordable housing needs of all Americans, including first-time buyers, the elderly, and those who need affordable rental housing.

WILMER, CUTLER & PICKERING

High quality work, responsiveness to client needs, challenging cases, dedication to the profession, collaborative teamwork, public service. The thirteen partners who founded Wilmer, Cutler & Pickering in 1962 believed these are the most important elements in the practice of law. Today, the more than 200 lawyers at the firm's offices in Washington, London, and Brussels continue to share these values.

The first priority at WC&P is to provide top-quality, responsive legal work—and successful results. Meeting the client's needs is basic; quality work is also a matter of intellectual fulfillment and professional pride. The firm has always acted principally as "lawyers' lawyers," helping clients solve unusual and high-stakes problems that raise difficult legal issues. In a survey by a national legal publication, corporate clients listed WC&P as one of a handful of

A WC&P partner in touch with a client.

firms to which they would turn if their company's very existence were at stake. The firm has offices in Brussels and London as well as Washington, and its cases frequently involve the U.S. government, the European community, or issues of federal or international law.

An advantage of a broadly diversified firm is the ability to assemble teams of experts in a variety of substantive areas that bear on the problems at hand. WC&P is organized into four broad practice areas covering many legal specialties. Reflecting the complex interrelationships of legal issues in matters the firm handles, many partners and associates belong to more than one practice area.

The Regulatory and Legislative practice includes the firm's antitrust, communications, computer law, consumer protection, environmental, energy, food and drug, government contracts, intellectual property, legislative, and occupational health and safety practice. This Washington-based national practice provides counseling and representation before state and federal courts, regulatory institutions, and the Congress.

The General Litigation practice is the center of the firm's trial and appellate litigation work, with specialities in commercial and

contractual disputes, insurance coverage, products liability, oil spill, and complex multi-party litigation. There is an active white-collar criminal practice. Lawyers in this group have conducted special investigations into alleged corporate misconduct, such as improper payments, foreign boycotts, and illegal campaign contributions.

The International practice handles international trade regulation, corporate and banking transactions, litigation, arbitration, aviation, telecommunications, and competition law, with a specialty in European Community regulation of a number of industries. Lawyers from Washington, London, and Brussels often work together as a team to resolve complex international matters.

The Corporate practice includes several related "clusters." The Securities Litigation and Enforcement cluster has one of the most active and diverse securities practices in the nation, including enforcement proceedings before the SEC and other agencies, private civil litigation, white-collar criminal work, and related broker-dealer regulatory and corporate counseling. The Corporate cluster handles business, commercial, and securities transactions, as well as mergers and acquisitions (including major contested acquisitions). The firm's Bankruptcy and Workout practice has included some of the largest and most complex insolvency proceedings in the country. The Banking cluster deals with a wide range of issues for bank and thrift institutions, including legislative and regulatory issues, failing institution problems, and litigation and enforcement matters. The Tax cluster handles tax planning, corporate and partnership transactions, IRS audit disputes, litigation, legislation, exempt organizations, ERISA, and tax aspects of bankruptcy.

The firm's lawyers strongly value public service. Lloyd Cutler was Counsel to President Carter. He is a member of the U.S. delegation to the Permanent Court of Arbitration and has worked on many presidential commissions and special assignments. John Pickering served as President of the D.C. Bar and has chaired many bar association and court-related bodies. Other partners have served as Deputy Solicitor General, United States Attorney, Attorney General of Maryland, and senior legal officials in the departments of Justice, State, Agriculture, Education, and the CIA, as well as counsel to committees of the Congress. Former partners serve or have served as federal judges,

A WC&P partner supervises a small team of young lawyers and legal assistants in preparing computer-graphic analyses of the facts in a major matter.

Counsel to President Bush, Corporation Counsel for the District of Columbia, and officers of major corporations.

The firm has a long and outstanding record of commitment to pro bono publico activities. The firm's pro bono program received the highest score in a 1990 survey of the 130 largest law firms in the U.S. It has received awards from the Litigation Section of the American Bar Association and many other groups. The firm's pro bono work is as diverse as the rest of its practice, often involving matters of considerable public interest.

Wilmer, Cutler & Pickering lawyers are backed by an excellent staff of almost 400 legal assistants, librarians, computer and graphics specialists, legislative specialists, and others. The firm strives to control client costs by lean staffing, reliance on appropriate nonlawyer support, and creative use of automation. In 1983 the firm made a then unprecedented decision to provide every lawyer with a personal computer. Today, everyone is linked by a Local Area Network, with instantaneous communication and access to files within and among the firm's offices. Many of the firm's clients are remotely linked to its electronic mail network. The firm's lawyers and computer specialists have developed a state-of-the-art system—including specialized data bases, optical imaging/text retrieval, and expert systems—to make their practice more efficient and powerful.

Top-quality, high-stakes legal work in a uniquely professional culture defines Wilmer, Cutler & Pickering and sets it apart. The firm remains a place where lawyers' principal concerns are meeting the most difficult and challenging needs of the client in a responsive and cost-effective way.

NATIONAL ASSOCIATION OF LIFE UNDERWRITERS

NALU's headquarters is located at 1922 F Street, N.W., in Washington. The building is a local landmark that was originally built to house the St. John's Orphanage.

The National Association of Life Underwriters (NALU) celebrated its centennial in 1990, marking 100 years of service to both consumers and professional life insurance agents throughout America. NALU, based in Washington, is among the oldest and largest trade associations in the insurance industry.

Nationwide, more than 142,000 career life insurance agents belong to local member associations affiliated with NALU. There are 950 local associations. These are linked with umbrella organizations in all 50 states, the District of Columbia, and Puerto Rico. Both state and local groups are affiliated with NALU.

NALU also hosts three affiliate groups or "conferences" : the Association of Health Insurance Agents, the Association for Advanced Life Underwriters, and the General Agents and Managers Association. All three are based at the NALU national headquarters building in Washington.

Since its inception, NALU has dedicated itself to improving the professionalism of life underwriters and improving public perceptions of professional life insurance agents. NALU views life insurance agents as financial advisors who can help clients achieve financial goals through skillful planning.

The association seeks to increase public awareness of the value of life insurance, both as a product and a service. NALU leaders note that the wide range of available policies and the complexity of many of them makes obtaining skilled, professional advice an absolute necessity. NALU advises the public to select a life insurance agent with care and attention.

"Your relationship with a life underwriter will be personal and confidential," advises NALU's executive vice president and chief executive officer Jack E. Bobo, CLU, FLMI. "You will certainly want to choose one on whom you can rely and who you feel will have continuing interest in you, your family, and your affairs." Bobo has served as chief executive officer since 1979. (CLU designates Chartered Life Underwriter and FLMI designates a Fellow of the Life Management Institution.)

NALU was formed in Boston by representatives of 14 regional associations. The Boston meeting marked the culmination of more than 20 years of organizational trial and error. It succeeded in an atmosphere of crisis. A growing trend toward unprofessional behavior threatened the entire industry. Practices eschewed by NALU pioneers included agents paying under-the-table rebates to stimulate profitable first-year sales and "twisting," or unjustified replacement of existing policies with new ones.

NALU was making limited progress when a full-fledged crisis hit the American life insurance industry. In 1906, stimulated by highly publicized financial abuses, the New York state legislature instituted a public investigation of the industry. The so-called "Armstrong Investigation" led to regulation of the industry, first in New York and then throughout the country.

The investigation increased public demand for the reforms that NALU had long advocated. As a result, President Theodore Roosevelt invited NALU president Charles Scovel to help draft a new national model insurance code. The model code was quickly adopted in many states.

Roosevelt's reliance on the NALU was not surprising. Then, as now, the NALU advocated policies and practices that benefited the public. The association has always recognized that the public interest and the interests of life insurance agents must always coincide. Then, too, as now, NALU was also intensely conscious of the need to educate the public to a full appreciation of life insurance.

NALU has also long been active in educating life insurance agents. The association began publishing its widely admired professional magazine, *Life Association News*, in 1906. The magazine has appeared regularly ever since. In 1915 the association published *Life Insurance: A Textbook by Solomon S. Huebner*, which soon became the profession's standard reference.

In 1927 NALU was instrumental in the founding of the American College of Life Underwriters and the establishment of the "Chartered Life Underwriter" designation as the industry's premier mark of professionalism. The association created the Million Dollar Round Table, the Life Underwriter Training Council, and other professional groups and marks of distinction.

Largely as a result of such efforts, the profession of life underwriting has continued to grow in prestige and profitability. Surveys by the Life Insurance Marketing and Research Association (LIMRA) demonstrate accelerating growth in the incomes of experienced, full-time career agents.

In recognition of the intimate relationships between life insurance agents and their communities, NALU has traditionally maintained active community support pro-

grams. The association believes strongly in demonstrating its public spirit and in "giving back to the community."

NALU's community outreach programs have been recognized nationally by many service organizations and by the White House. In 1988 and 1989 President Ronald Reagan honored NALU with the distinguished Presidential Award, one of only 30 such awards presented each year for outstanding community service. Since 1984 NALU and 75 of its state and local associations have been honored for community service as part of former President Reagan's Citation Program for Private Sector Initiatives. In 1991 the American Society of Associate Executives presented NALU with its Summit Award for volunteerism.

NALU has its national headquarters at 1922 F Street, N.W., in Washington, D.C., a local landmark originally built to house the St. John's Orphanage. NALU purchased the building in 1959 for $516,000. It added a new wing in 1979, and renovated the interior in 1990. It shares the building with the District of Columbia Life Underwriters Association and its three conferences.

In 1990 the National Association of Life Underwriters celebrated its 100th anniversary.

EPSTEIN BECKER & GREEN

Founded in 1973, the law firm of Epstein Becker & Green has placed itself among the nation's legal elite in health law, labor and employment, corporate securities, government procurement, and related fields.

With roots in New York and Washington, the firm has assumed a national presence. It now has offices in San Francisco, Los Angeles, Dallas, Miami, Boston, and several other major cities. A network of corresponding and affiliated firms around the world makes Epstein Becker & Green an active player on the international scene as well.

Its pioneering role in the field of health law and its breadth of experience in labor and employment law has made Epstein Becker a leading force in those specialties. "In many ways they are overlapping areas," says Doug Hastings, a health and hospital law specialist and member of the firm's Washington office.

"Health care has become a vital issue, equally important to employers and health care providers. Our experience in both employment law and health law allows us to implement new strategies successfully with a minimum of risk."

Its pioneering employment and health departments have made Epstein Becker the national firm of choice dealing with mergers of health care institutions. "There's a lot more to hospital mergers than the legal side," says founding partner Steven B. Epstein. "You have to see what that organization is going to look like after the hospitals have merged. You have to have a vision of what this entity—and the industry—will look like in five years."

"Our full range of clients allows us to see the health care industry as a whole, to see where it's headed," adds William Kopit, a senior member of the health law section in the Washington office and the firm's leading expert on antitrust issues.

That "vision" has won widespread respect and professional success. The firm represents more than 200 of the *Fortune* 500 industrial corporations; it has represented the American Hospital Association before the United States Supreme Court.

Epstein is senior health partner in the firm's Washington office. He is a graduate of Tufts University and Columbia University Law School. Before starting his firm, he was a consultant at the United States Department of Health, Education, and Welfare.

Cofounder Jeffrey H. Becker is the firm's senior New York health law partner. A gradu-

ate of Brown University, he is a former editor of the *New York University Law Review*.

Ronald M. Green, the firm's senior labor and employment law litigator, heads the employment law department and is resident in the New York office. Before joining the firm, he served as chief counsel for civil rights and associate solicitor of labor for labor relations and civil rights with the Department of Labor.

"Before 1965," says Epstein, "a 'health care' lawyer either did malpractice work or perhaps helped out a local client. Then came Medicare, and the explosion of health care from a profession into an industry, and all the regulatory follow-up."

"We represent every piece of the health care industry in all of its corporate entities," says Becker. "That includes health care providers, health care insurers, and employers. We deal with financial and ethical issues. We seek to fulfill long-term values and objectives. We look for good business concepts as the foundation for any program."

An appreciation of such values made it possible for the firm to help Carilion Health System complete an important merger of two hospitals in Roanoke, Virginia. The merger was accomplished, despite a challenge by the U.S. Department of Justice, after Epstein Becker and the hospitals were able to demonstrate the significant benefit to the community which would result from the merger.

The firm's labor law practice is similarly involved in resolving complex issues. Over the past 20 years, Epstein Becker & Green has developed remarkable expertise in the constantly shifting environment shaped by changing civil rights, antidiscrimination, and immigration law.

The firm has also developed expertise in the related areas of substance-abuse testing, trade-secret matters, ERISA, affirmative action, and family issues. (Other independent departments deal with government contracts and legislative affairs.)

"We provide solutions, not problems," says Epstein. "That's really the foundation of our entire practice. We prefer to work on the front end as advisors and consultants. We'd rather accomplish 85 percent of a client's goals tomorrow, instead of 100 percent after years of litigation and delay. Of course we also have an outstanding litigation department backing us up." The Epstein Becker & Green litigation department operates both in conjunction with other groups and independently.

In all, Epstein Becker & Green offers 14 departments: Benefits, Construction, Corporate, Election/Lobbying, Employment, Government Contracts, Health, Immigration, Labor, Litigation, Real Estate, Securities, Tax, and Trusts & Estates.

"We've been successful because we've pioneered new approaches to legal counseling," says Hastings. "We use a team approach. We have a fully integrated office staff. Everyone here is constantly aware of the others' work. We all contribute. We all seek advice from each other."

Epstein Becker & Green attorneys have made their counsel widely available to the international legal community through hundreds of articles appearing in professional journals and other publications. The firm also offers various legal seminars throughout the country and publishes several newsletters, including the widely respected *Epstein Becker Report on Health Law.*

Above: Founding partner Steven B. Epstein (left) confers with partners Douglas A. Hastings (center) and Kenneth B. Weckstein on the steps of the U.S. Capitol.

HOWREY & SIMON

The offices of the Washington law firm of Howrey & Simon overlook the White House. However, this 35-year-old Washington firm has more than a great view. From its original base, Howrey & Simon has expanded its scope of services to include expertise in:

- Antitrust
- Commercial Litigation
- Environmental
- Government Contracts
- Insurance Coverage
- Intellectual Property
- International Trade
- Products Liability
- Security Litigation
- White-Collar Criminal Defense

With more than 225 attorneys on staff, Howrey & Simon is among the fastest growing law firms in the country.

Tough assignments from the world's leading companies
The courtroom and conference-table skills of the lawyers of Howrey & Simon have attracted an impressive client list. A selection of some of its better known clients includes:

- AB SKF Group Companies
- Anheuser-Busch Companies, Inc.
- Armco Inc.

- Armstrong World Industries Inc.
- Ashland Oil Inc.
- Bayer/Mobay Group Companies
- Calvin Klein Cosmetics Corporation
- Capital Holding Corporation
- Carolina Power & Light Company
- Caterpillar Inc.
- COMSAT
- Crown Central Petroleum Corporation
- Cyprus Minerals Company
- Dana Corporation
- Encyclopaedia Britannica, Inc.
- Exxon Corporation
- General Mills, Inc.
- Hanson Industries
- H.J. Heinz Company
- Hershey Foods Corporation
- Heublein, Inc.
- Huffy Corporation
- Intel Corporation
- Johnson & Johnson
- Johnson Controls, Inc.
- Litton Industries, Inc.
- The LTV Corporation
- Martin Marietta Corporation
- McDonnell Douglas
- MCI
- The Mead Corporation
- Minnesota Mining and Manufacturing Company (3M)
- Mobil Corporation
- Nestle Companies
- Owens-Illinois Inc.
- Parker Hannifin Corp.

- PepsiCo, Inc.
- The Quaker Oats Company
- Rockwell International Corporation
- Schering-Plough Corporation
- Shell Oil Company
- Siemens AG (Germany)
- Teledyne, Inc.
- Texas Instruments Incorporated
- Timex Corporation
- Unilever United States, Inc.
- Unisys Corp.
- Wang Laboratories, Inc.

To support its litigators, Howrey & Simon has created two subsidiary firms, Capital Accounting and Capital Economics. The subsidiaries have become centers of excellence in their own right, providing clients with consultation and analysis involving litigation and regulatory matters.

Increased effectiveness through litigation technology
Howrey & Simon has made substantial investments in technology:

- State-of-the-art document imaging enhances the firm's ability to provide a competitive litigation edge at competitive costs.

- High speed data and voice communication maximizes the effectiveness of staff working at client locations, no matter how remote or distant they may be.

In 1992 Howrey & Simon opened an office in Los Angeles, California, and merged with the firm of Hennigan & Mercer. The new office enables the firm to provide more efficient service to its West Coast and Pacific Rim clients.

WILKES, ARTIS, HEDRICK & LANE, CHARTERED

Right: The Intelsat headquarters of the U.S. State Department's international center project.

Below: The Geico headquarters in Friendship Heights/Chevy Chase, Maryland.

For more than 66 years Wilkes, Artis, Hedrick & Lane, Chartered, has proudly played a major role in shaping and developing the Washington metropolitan area. From Federal Triangle to Georgetown, from the Southwest waterfront to Montgomery Village, the firm has been involved in planning and problem-solving, action, and achievement.

With more than 67 attorneys and professional staff, and offices in the District of Columbia, Bethesda, Maryland, and Fairfax, Virginia, the present firm combines the legal practices and expertise of two well-established Washington, D.C., law firms: Wilkes & Artis and Hedrick & Lane.

Beginning in 1926, Wilkes & Artis engaged in the general practice of law in the District of Columbia and throughout the area. As the needs of its clients grew, the firm established offices in suburban Maryland and Virginia. The firm became well known for its expertise in real estate law, including zoning, condemnation, real property tax assessment, urban planning and redevelopment, historic preservation, construction and permanent financing, and the shaping of local legislation. In addition, the firm has advised corporate clients across the country in sophisticated business matters and in the complex area of environmental regulations, which have increasingly restricted the use, sale, and development of real estate.

The District of Columbia and the Washington metropolitan

area have changed dramatically in the past 60 years. Wilkes, Artis, Hedrick & Lane has been responsible for many of those changes: the zoning for and development of the downtown business area, the Connecticut Avenue and Wisconsin Avenue corridors, the Southwest Urban Renewal area, the Pennsylvania Avenue and West End development areas, METRO, and the Convention Center.

The firm has been intimately involved in various aspects of planning, development, and financing for Georgetown, Catholic, American, and George Washington universities, Trinity College, and Children's Hospital. The firm has been involved in Pennsylvania Avenue redevelopment projects such as the Willard Hotel and in the creation of the first condominium in Washington, Tiber Island. It has also left its imprint on such suburban projects as Montgomery Village, Chevy Chase Pavillion,

Rock Spring Center, Mazza Gallerie, and GEICO's headquarters in Maryland and Skyline Towers and Lincoln Place in Virginia.

In 1982 Wilkes & Artis merged with the firm of Hedrick & Lane, which specialized in the federal regulatory, administrative, tax, and legislative areas. Since that time the firm has also become heavily involved in the telecommunications field, as well as government contracting and procurement, taxation, litigation, patent infringement and trademark matters, and international trade.

Accomplishments in these practice areas have included obtaining major radio frequency allocations for public safety agencies, establishing for the first time a minority preference in broadcast licensing decisions, the

successful advocacy of "reasonable access" to the broadcast media for presidential candidates during political campaigns, and the successful defense of major contractors involved in the navy nuclear program. The firm also specializes in creating public safety networks for municipal police, fire, and emergency medical departments nationwide.

Within the Washington region, Wilkes, Artis, Hedrick & Lane handles an impressive portfolio of the administrative and judicial appeals of commercial real property tax assessments. The firm's insight into factors affecting property values, operating expenses, and capitalization rates has proven effective for its clients' interests.

The firm's litigation practice encompasses the full range of property-related matters as well as concentrated experience in commercial litigation and complex trial matters. Cases involving patent and trademark infringement, contract disputes, medical malpractice, and product liability have also been tried.

During the past decade, the firm's practice has expanded to include a skilled group of tax and estate planning attorneys. This practice area advises clients on issues involving franchise and other privilege taxes, mergers and acquisitions, incorporations, reorganizations and liquidations, federal and state income taxes, as well as gift and estate taxes.

Because of their institutional knowledge and experience, Wilkes, Artis, Hedrick & Lane attorneys bring insights and intelli-

gence to the vigorous interplay of the national capital region. They actively participate on the policy making boards of business and professional organizations and have contributed their time and efforts to community needs and organizations.

As the needs of the region and the country continue to expand, the firm will be as involved in the future as it has been in shaping the past. Wilkes, Artis, Hedrick & Lane values its associations with the people who have made the firm's development possible and intends to nurture these friendships and establish new ones as it moves toward the next century.

Chapter Eight

INDUSTRY AND HIGH TECHNOLOGY

. . . .

A Region Broadens Its Horizons

The capital region's centralized location and qualified work force attract manufacturers and high-tech industries to the area.

Photo by Matthew Borkoski/Folio

SIGAL CONSTRUCTION

Right: Pennsylvania Plaza is one of the first major mixed-use complexes just a few blocks from the Capitol, combining 170,000 square feet of office and retail space and 150 residences above 3 levels of below-grade parking. Photo by Carol Highsmith and David Patterson

Below right: The headquarters office for The Discovery Channel, a major cable television company, is one of many broadcast and telecommunications facilities built by SIGAL. Photo by Prakash Patel

When it comes to making the cosmopolitan "new" Washington fit in with the city's traditional architecture, the general contractor of choice is frequently SIGAL Construction. The firm is equally noted for new construction, interiors, and renovation work. The "SIGAL" banner on a job site has become widely recognized throughout the industry as a symbol of top-quality construction.

SIGAL's award-winning renovation projects include the Evening Star building on Pennsylvania Avenue, the Manhattan Laundry, and the historic Bond Building, just two blocks from the White House. The firm's new construction projects enrich skylines throughout the national capital region.

Based in downtown Washington, SIGAL is one of Washington's largest and most active locally owned and operated construction contractors. To better control its projects, the company confines its activities to its home region. Most SIGAL projects lie within a short drive of the main office on Georgetown's Potomac riverfront.

The company's founder, Gerald R. Sigal, has been in the construction business since he joined New York's Tishman Realty and Construction as a teenage laborer. In 1971 Tishman appointed Gerry Sigal as project manager for the World Trade Center. He came to Washington to manage Tishman's Washington office and lead the construction team at Georgetown's Foundry.

In 1977 Sigal turned down the opportunity to be project manager for Walt Disney World's EPCOT Center. He chose, instead, to stay in Washington and start his own company. He founded SIGAL Construction with a total capital investment of $2,200 and the

close, active support of his wife, Ellen.

"Our first job was the Earl Allen Tennis Shop," recalls Sigal. "I was the superintendent and project manager, and when the guys left at 3:30, I swept the floors." Five years later SIGAL Construction headed *Inc.* magazine's list of the nation's 500 most rapidly growing firms. By 1986 SIGAL Construction was an $80-million-a-year business. In 1990 Gerry Sigal was nominated by Ernst & Young as Entrepreneur of the Year.

In 1984 Joseph A. (Jeb) Turner III, who previously directed the Washington office of Turner Construction, joined SIGAL as chief operating officer. He was subsequently named president.

SIGAL specializes in commercial, corporate, and institutional construction. It has two operating divisions: one for new construction, the other for renovation and interior construction. The building division accounted for most of the firm's rapid early growth. SIGAL's recent growth has been evenly shared by the two operating units.

Together, the two divisions have made SIGAL Construction one of Washington's most widely admired, publicized, and recognized construction firms. In 1988 *Building Design and Construction* magazine published a lengthy profile of the company. In 1990 the firm's work on the Evening Star building renovation won cover-story treatment from *Buildings* magazine. The same project has also won numerous awards in international competition.

"Construction is a good business," says Turner. "It's honest, visible, three-dimensional. It's exciting. It's a business people can understand, one that people love to watch. That's why our site fences have holes in them."

"Construction has energy and drama," says Sigal. "This company reflects that in its people and the way we do business. Our corporate culture focuses on creatively channeling that energy. We've created a web of networks stretching across traditional departmental lines. All of our people understand how their work impacts others."

"People want to be part of a community," says Turner. "They want to feel good about their jobs. They want to feel secure. They want to understand what they're doing. The more training we provide, the more these things happen." SIGAL starts its training of new employees with a 750-page manual, and follows up with seminars by experts drawn from throughout the building trades.

SIGAL also offers seminars for clients, designers, brokers, and other outside parties. These programs help support the firm's cooperative atmosphere. They also help the people who work with SIGAL understand the company's unique corporate culture.

The success of SIGAL Construction's way of doing business is visible throughout the region. Among the company's best-known projects: Pennsylvania Plaza, the new MCI World Headquarters Building, and the Evening Star building, all on Pennsylvania Avenue; Arlington Square, the Bell Atlantic Network Services Building, Sequoia Plaza, the main offices for Gannett Corporation and USA Today, and headquarters offices for the Drug Enforcement Administration and U.S. Marshals Service, all in Arlington; The Bond Building, The Portal Building, Jefferson Court, Gallery Row, and many other office buildings in Washington; Research Office Center and Two White Flint North in Maryland; and numerous educational facilities for such clients as Mount Vernon College and Georgetown Day School.

The company's success with major, high-profile buildings has not kept it from continuing its involvement with smaller, less-visible projects. "Even if you're just putting in a single piece of drywall," says Turner, "it ought to be straight, the joints should be well taped, and the finish, even if it's just paint, should be perfect. We're known for our quality, but we don't only do expensive work. We build at all levels."

SIGAL Construction has shared its success with the Washington community and makes community involvement a high priority within the company. Its staff plays a leading role at many regional and national civic, cultural, and charitable activities, including Christmas in April, Big Brothers, the Leukemia Society of America, the Easter Seals Society, the Duke University Comprehensive Cancer Center, and many others.

TURNER CONSTRUCTION

Above: The 2,000-seat Performing Arts Center at George Mason University in Fairfax, Virginia, is really several theaters in one, with state-of-the-art facilities that make it suitable for a wide range of performances. Photo by Steve Gottlieb Photography

Right: Clear spans from exterior wall to central core are a feature of the 400,000-square-foot Homart Tysons II office building, which Turner built using the flying form technique of construction.

Since 1902, the nation's largest general contractor has been guided by three simple words: "Service, service, service." Turner's strong presence nationwide and in the Washington, D.C., metropolitan area is a testimony to how well the company has followed its own advice during its 90-year history.

Turner Construction is responsible for building some of the most challenging structures in the nation. They include major corporate headquarters buildings, stadiums, convention centers, hotels, and health care facilities. In Washington, the company's presence dates back to World War I, and recently has included such projects as the new center for the performing arts at George Mason University, the Prince Georges County Courthouse, and the Tysons II Office Tower.

Service is the common thread that runs through all these projects. As the premier health care, educational, and institutional builder in the Washington area, Turner has conscientiously solicited work on the basis of an extraordinarily close and supportive relationship with its clients. More than 60 percent of the company's business is from repeat customers, and more than 70 percent is negotiated work.

According to J. Glenn Little, Washington, D.C., vice president and general manager, "Our philosophy is reflected in the process that we use to obtain and execute work. In all our projects, we strive to provide the highest possible value at the lowest cost to the client. Good communication and an aggressive approach to quality and service have consistently positioned us to deliver that value."

Health care clients put a premium on quality and service. Turner's reputation for both has enabled it to maintain the highest volume of health care work of any contractor in the Washington area. Fairfax, Arlington, and Georgetown hospitals have contracted with Turner time and again to perform renovations and additions, which are made more challenging by the fact that the facilities must remain in operation during construction. The company's health care expertise has also been recognized by Chesapeake and DePaul hospitals and the University of Maryland medical system. Currently, Turner has also worked on the expansion of American Medical Labs recently completed in Chantilly, Virginia.

Whether the project is commercial or institutional, Turner delivers the same coordinated approach to project management. The estimating, purchasing, and sales depart-

ments provide a comprehensive range of services; exhaustive preconstruction budgeting and aggressive procurement help clients obtain the right structure for the right price. During preconstruction, Turner proactively participates in the design process, helping both the owner and the architects to develop viable alternative design scenarios. Once the project is ready to roll, operations steps in with logistical plans and scheduling. The field staff works with the owner and architect to determine the most economical and expeditious method of construction. Turner also provides tenant buildout services through its Special Projects Division, often in conjunction with major office tower projects.

The Washington office, which was established in 1975, is supported by a nationwide construction network. With 2,850 employees and a presence in 100 cities nationwide, Turner has expertise in every type of construction, and can dedicate a wealth of resources to assure the quality of projects in any part of the country.

In the final analysis, however, the quality of a company's work can only be as good as the personnel who perform it. Business development manager Tom Paci attributes much of Turner's success to its superior staff. "Most of our people join Turner right out of college and spend their entire professional lives with us. We invest in their careers. They are career-oriented, but they also recognize that the success of a project is a function of the effort put forth by the entire team."

In fact, Turner's dedication to team-building has given it a reputation throughout the industry. The company has been widely recognized for setting the industry standard in affirmative action and minority business programs. It has been nationally recognized for encouragement of small and disadvantaged businesses, a fact which has not gone unnoticed by the public sector. The Prince Georges County Justice Center, a $70-million project, was recently completed by the association of Turner and Precision Contractors, a 100 percent minority-owned firm.

Minority opportunity is one part of Turner's long-standing commitment to community involvement; staff members in the Washington area find time to make a variety of contributions. The fifth semester of the Contractor's College, a six-week college level seminar of construction topics, was presented by Turner employees and selected outside experts in spring 1992. Howard University

and the District government were co-sponsors. General manager J. Glenn Little is an active fund-raising member of the Cystic Fibrosis board and the properties committee of the Salvation Army Board, among others. Other Turner staffers host the Christ House soup kitchen and participate in the Associated General Contractors (AGC) and Career Real Estate Women (CREW), two professional organizations.

When Glenn Little says that "quality is not a cliche at Turner," he means that attention to quality is more than a catch phrase. It permeates every aspect of the company's operation, from the performance of each team member to the role that the company plays as a corporate citizen in the community.

Below: The Prince Georges County Courthouse, a 356,000-square-foot, $70-million project, was completed on time and under budget by Turner in association with a minority partner. Photo by Steve Gottlieb Photography

Left: The 300,000-square-foot addition to Fairfax Hospital is Turner's third project for this client. The $37-million project was completed while the hospital remained fully occupied and operational. Photo by Steve Gottlieb Photography

CACI

To many, what makes or breaks a high-tech company is technology, state-of-the-art facilities, or even marketing campaigns. But to Jack P. London, the chairman, president, and chief executive officer of CACI—an international information systems and high-technology services corporation based in Arlington, Virginia—a high-tech company's greatest asset is always its people.

"When I first joined CACI, our corporate strategy was determined by the need to meet next week's payroll," says London, reminiscing about 1972. "We thrived because we had a skilled, productive, fun group of people who enjoyed professionalism and hard work. Since then we've learned a lot about building a company and positioning it to best take advantage of the world around us and the future ahead. But we still know that it's our people who really make the difference."

Founded in 1962 by the creators of SIM-SCRIPT II.5®, still the world's premier computer simulation language, CACI now has offices throughout America and Western Europe and a distinguished, international client list that includes major agencies of na-

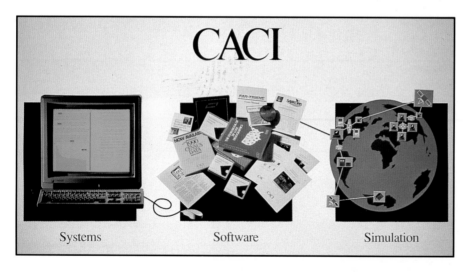

CACI

| Systems | Software | Simulation |

tional governments and the *Fortune* 500.

With 1991 gross revenues of $136 million, CACI is among the elite of the providers of systems integration, software services, and products to the international community. The company is best known for information systems, simulation, and international marketing systems.

"You've got to scout the world for technological developments," observes London. "We have technologically oriented people and we make it a point to know where technology is going and how to bring it to our clients. Not being an equipment manufacturer, we are

free to develop the integrated solution that best fits a client's needs and pocketbook."

A graduate of the U.S. Naval Academy and former naval aviator, London holds a master of science in operations research from the Navy's Post Graduate School and a doctor of business administration "with distinction" from George Washington University. He—like CACI itself and its other executives—is active in the Washington community. He has served on the Professional Services Council's board of directors and is a member of the George Washington University Alumni Association, the U.S. Naval Academy Alumni Association, and the Naval Institute.

The mission statement guiding CACI's people challenges them to make the company a "world leader in advanced information technology solutions." This means delivering "high user-value" systems and services, a challenge London believes can be met because of the company's particular blend of technical experience, creativity, and expertise.

CACI's private- and government-sector clients span defense, aerospace, communications, transportation, finance, real estate, litigation, retail, and more. And the company insists that its solutions meet not only the current needs of these diverse clients, but also future needs—what CACI calls "technology with tomorrow in mind."

One of London's own greatest challenges is to keep his people exploring—searching for relevant areas in which to expand the company's services, products, and markets. "We can't help our clients build their futures," he says, "if we don't build our own."

VEGA PRECISION LABORATORIES

Established in 1963, VEGA Precision Laboratories is a leader in the radar-enhancement field. The firm designs and manufactures sophisticated electronics products for the U.S. and foreign governments, and for private industry. At its secluded complex not far from downtown Vienna, Virginia, VEGA has complete facilities and staff for engineering, design, development, production, and testing of all of its products.

VEGA products include electronic equipment, ranging from radar transponders and antennas to highly-specialized, U.A.V. Command and Control systems, requiring telemetry data link equipment, and digital logic circuitry.

VEGA's products and systems are based on precise measurements of time and detection of electromagnetic radiation. The combination makes it possible for VEGA to create highly-advanced radar systems and related technologies.

VEGA manufactures many of its products in transportable and portable versions. The VEGA portable radar tracker, one of the company's ruggedized products, has been widely acclaimed by customers.

VEGA customers range from NASA and the Federal Aviation Administration to all five armed services, leading research universities, and major American and foreign aerospace manufacturers. Several items of VEGA-designed and -built equipment recently saw field use in the Persian Gulf, such as a VEGA system that was used to test and evaluate the Patriot missile during its evaluation and test phase.

VEGA-designed systems also allow the control of sub-scale and full-size unmanned aircraft. VEGA systems have been installed at Tyndall Air Force Base in Florida, at White Sands Missile Range in New Mexico, and at Wallace Air Station in the Philippines. Transportable models of the system have been purchased by the U.S. Army and several foreign governments for use on their test ranges.

Another important application of the VEGA command and data system is in "flight termination." Flight-termination systems provide a fail-safe means to destroy test missiles that deviate from programmed flight plans. VEGA's Flight Termination System has been used on the AMRAAM and WASP missiles.

Many VEGA products have also found popular civilian applications. VEGA systems are used with weather radar on helicopters to assist oil company geological exploration

Left: M.C. (Tony) Barnard, president, VEGA Precision Laboratories.

Below: VEGA Precision Laboratories.

teams. One system has recently found an even more unlikely use. It has become the premier fish-finding and -tracking radar system used by international fishing fleets.

VEGA has 190 employees at its Vienna complex. Tony Barnard is president of VEGA and its parent company, Carlton Industries. Ed Webber is executive vice president. Marketing vice presidents are Jay LeVan and Bill Kinsley for International. Joe Bennett is director of National Business.

VEGA generates annual sales of approximately $20 million. With customers in more than 14 foreign countries, more than half of VEGA's sales are in the international arena. The company has representatives throughout Europe, and in Australia, Japan, India, Korea, Pakistan, Singapore, and Taiwan.

FAIRCHILD CORPORATION

The Fairchild Corporation, based in Chantilly, Virginia, on the grounds of Washington Dulles International Airport, is a leading worldwide supplier of specialized aerospace and industrial components. It is also a participant in the telecommunications market. A diversified organization, Fairchild's principal operations include total or partial ownership of: the Fairchild Fastener Group, D-M-E Company, Fairchild Communications Services Company, Banner Aerospace, Inc., and Rexnord Corporation.

Right: D-M-E's commitment to quality, technology, leadership, delivery, and cost is the reason it was awarded General Motors "Mark of Excellence" Award, the most prestigious in the industry.

Far right: Since its founding in 1985, Fairchild Communications Services has become the market leader in providing centralized telecommunications services for commercial office buildings throughout the United States.

Below: Fairchild Fastener Group accounts for more than 30 percent of aerospace fastener manufacturing worldwide. All fasteners are engineered for specific aircraft applications and manufactured to strict tolerances.

Fairchild Industries traces its origins to 1920, when Sherman Fairchild patented the first automatic aerial camera with a between-the-lens shutter. To develop, manufacture, and market his invention, he formed the Fairchild Aerial Camera Corporation in New York.

To exploit commercial use of the camera, Fairchild founded aerial survey companies in Canada and the United States. To meet the needs of his survey companies, Fairchild built his own airplanes and engines.

Fairchild's first production airplane established his company as America's largest supplier of civil transport aircraft. Fairchild went on to develop many successful civilian and military aircraft, including the P-47 Thunderbolt, the F-105 Thunderchief, and the A-10 Thunderbolt II.

Fairchild discontinued its airframe business in 1987 but continued to operate a substantial aircraft fastener business. Fairchild merged with Banner Industries, another diversified aerospace parts manufacturer, in

1989. Banner, a Cleveland-based company, was founded in 1956. Through several acquisitions, Banner owned a wide array of industrial and aerospace businesses. In 1990, reflecting further evolution of the company and the proud heritage of the Fairchild name, Banner changed its name to The Fairchild Corporation.

Fairchild Fastener Group: As the premier company in its industry, Fairchild accounts for more than 30 percent of the worldwide production of aerospace fasteners. Fairchild customers are involved in most commercial and military aerospace programs around the world. The group employs more than 2,000 people at 18 facilities in 6 countries.

D-M-E Company: The world leader in the manufacture of tooling and electronic control systems for the plastics injection molding industry. The sales, distribution, and technical services network of D-M-E extends to 37

countries supplying products to 60 nations. D-M-E also integrates and distributes its own computer-aided design and manufacturing system, fully customized to plastics injection molding applications.

Fairchild Communications Services: Fairchild provides office buildings with integrated systems including digital switching, telephone equipment, and long-distance (including international) calling services. The company has successfully capitalized on opportunities resulting from the deregulated U.S. telecommunications environment. With revenues nearing the $60-million milestone, Fairchild Communications has become the country's leading provider of centralized telecommunications services.

Rexnord Corporation: Rexnord is a leading manufacturer of mechanical power transmission components. Its products are used throughout the world, in virtually every industry, including food and beverage processing, aerospace, construction, energy, and agriculture, among many others. Fairchild owns 45 percent of Rexnord Corporation, a publicly owned company.

Banner Aerospace: Fairchild continues to own 47 percent of Banner Aerospace, a publicly owned company since August 1990. Banner Aerospace comprises the former Aerospace Distribution Group of Banner Industries. It is among the world's leading distributors of replacement parts to the aviation aftermarket.

"Our strategy is to enhance the inherent value of each of our businesses by investing in areas that will sharpen their competitive edges," says Jeffrey J. Steiner, chairman, president, and chief executive officer of The Fairchild Corporation. "We will also continue efforts to find viable international joint ven-

tures which will enable us to penetrate new global markets."

Born in Austria, Steiner is chairman of the board of governors of Haifa University in Israel and a trustee of Montefiore Medical Center in New York. He has been honored by the governments of France and Italy. Steiner is also a member of the boards of Rexnord Corporation, Banner Aerospace, Inc., Fairchild Industries, Inc., The Copley Fund, and the Franklin Corporation.

"We have strong assets to build shareholder value," says Steiner. "We have world-class businesses whose product lines are in expanding markets. We have footholds in countries around the world which will help us to realize greater global business opportunities. And we have the financial strength to invest in our businesses, and experienced managers and employees whose commitment and skills will help make it happen."

Above: Banner Aerospace's commitment to maintaining a high level of service is demonstrated by its computerized inventory systems and its close proximity to various international airports, both of which facilitate response to customer needs within 24 hours.

Above left: Rexnord, a leading manufacturer of mechanical power transmission components, maintains its global market leadership by constantly developing innovative products while adhering to the strictest levels of quality control.

WESTAT

Westat, based in Rockville, Maryland, is an employee-owned contract research organization. Its clients are U.S. government agencies and a broad range of institutions and businesses. Its studies and surveys are used by researchers and policymakers to plan and evaluate programs in many different governmental areas, such as health care delivery and financing, educational achievement, job training, and military recruitment.

Major projects include epidemiologic studies and clinical trials to gain new understanding of the causes of disease and the efficacy of treatments, surveys to estimate the incidence of child abuse and maltreatment, biomedical research relating to the safety of the nation's blood supply, and analyses of environmental risk from toxic substances and hazardous waste. Some projects have taken Westat staff abroad to implement international data collections in collaboration with foreign governments and to train industrial organizations in statistical methods for quality control.

Westat's professional research staff of 500 includes senior statisticians who are internationally recognized as authorities in sample survey design, as well as psychologists, medical researchers, sociologists, economists, computer systems analysts, and programmers. They design surveys, apply modern quantitative and qualitative research methods, and provide clients with detailed analyses of results. They have technical expertise in computerized data systems and have extensive experience in many governmental program areas. The Crossley Surveys staff in New York City specializes in commercial market research.

A staff of supervisors and interviewers throughout the country and three telephone interviewing centers in Maryland and California make Westat one of the largest survey organizations in the United States. Its computer center in Rockville links to a micro-computer network and supports statistical analysis as well as computer-assisted data collection from both telephone and in-person interviews.

Employee ownership has helped Westat attract an outstanding staff and has played a vital part in the company's success. It motivates employees and gives Westat the freedom and incentive to build new capabilities with long-term investments.

From 1986 to 1991 Westat's staff and revenues have more than doubled. This growth reflects the increasing importance of accurate and timely information in research and governmental operations. And it also reflects the skill and experience of Westat's staff and its reputation for high-quality technical performance.

MAXIMA CORPORATION

From its headquarters in Prince Georges County, MAXIMA Corporation operates one of America's most successful broad-based information-management services and technology companies. Its clients include both Prince Georges and Montgomery county governments, numerous federal agencies, and other public agencies and private-sector corporations throughout the nation.

MAXIMA's record of achievement has won recognition from *Inc.* magazine, *Black Enterprise, Tempo, Capital,* the city of Baltimore, and the state of Maryland.

Founded in 1978 by Joshua Smith, the company now has more than 750 employees, with offices and projects in 13 states, and annual sales exceeding $45 million. Even a brief sampling of its projects list is impressive. MAXIMA manages the central and divi-

That commitment to excellence traces to MAXIMA's founder and chief executive officer, Joshua Smith, one of America's most widely recognized and respected minority entrepreneurs. As chairman of the U.S. Commission on Minority Business Development, Smith travels the country, challenging government, business, and citizens to recognize the value of minority business.

"I strongly believe that business in a capitalistic society is the fuel to freedom," says Smith. "If you don't have a strong economy, you don't have a strong anything."

MAXIMA is strong enough to put Smith on Regardie's list of the 100 most powerful businesspeople in Washington. It is also strong enough to make him a welcome visitor to Kuwait in the wake of the war in the Persian Gulf.

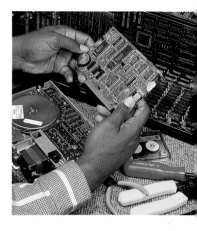

Above: Maxima hardware maintenance.

Left: Maxima facility operation.

sion document rooms for the Food and Drug Administration, maintains personnel files for the National Institutes of Health, and maintains the nuclear document system for the Nuclear Regulatory Commission.

MAXIMA also provides a broad range of information management and support services to corporate clients throughout the country. A commitment to excellence motivates the entire organization. That commitment has been recognized by MAXIMA's customers. The company's growth over the past 14 years is based largely on repeat business and a reputation for industry-leading quality.

MAXIMA Corporation concentrates on four business areas: systems engineering and integration, computer facilities management, information/records management, and telecommunications support network/services. "We're in services," says Smith. "We know what we are and what we're not. We know that we can't be all things to all people.'

In addition to its national headquarters in Lanham, the company operates major units in Oak Ridge, Tennessee; Redlands, California; at Wright-Patterson Air Force Base in Dayton, Ohio; and in Montgomery County and Prince Georges County, Maryland.

SOFTWARE AG

Right: Software AG: Solutions Worldwide

Below: Software AG: Worldwide Headquarters

With the advent of the information age in the 1970s and 1980s, access to data became a critical element, often determining

the success of an organization. Then, as now, timely information is the strategic weapon in the battle for market share. A leader of innovative information technology since the early days of the computer industry, SOFTWARE AG has become one of the world's largest independent systems software firms.

SOFTWARE AG specializes in software tools and services that solve a wide range of business and information management problems. The large-scale operational and business application development arena—manufacturing, banking, federal and state government, and airline reservation systems, for example—is the company's strength. Its products lead their markets in

many countries, including the United States, Japan, Germany, Australia, Brazil, and Spain.

Truly a global organization, SOFTWARE AG is headquartered in both Reston, Virginia, and Darmstadt, Germany. Founded in 1969, the company has been a pioneer in the evolution of computer technology. It maintains its technological edge by reinvesting 25 percent of revenues into product development, marking it as a leader among software companies in R&D investment. "That's how we continually provide our customers with the most advanced business solutions," says Michael J. King, president and CEO of SOFTWARE AG of North America.

SOFTWARE AG Federal Systems was formed in 1987 to acknowledge the unique business and information needs of the federal government. Its charter is to support and market SOFTWARE AG products to the federal government, contractors, and integrators in the federal market sector. Today, more than 110 installation sites exist in both civilian and military agencies. NASA, the FAA, the FBI, and the EPA are among the many organizations that have come to depend on SOFTWARE AG as a trusted partner.

During the Persian Gulf war, SOFTWARE AG Federal Systems worked overtime in cooperation with the U.S. Marine Corps. The goal: to establish Force Automated Services Centers (FASCs) in Saudi Arabia. Two FASCs were in operation just 30 days after the departure orders were cut. The FASCs rely on applications written in ADABAS® and NATURAL®, SOFTWARE AG's flagship products.

ADABAS was introduced in 1971 as a high-performance, on-line transaction processing (OLTP) database management system. Its ability to meet data management needs has proven the test of time, receiving the highest user satisfaction ratings in a recent independent survey by *Computerworld* magazine (August 17, 1992).

Building on the success of ADABAS, SOFTWARE AG introduced NATURAL in 1979.

SOFTWARE AG
Worldwide Corporation Operational Responsibilities

Worldwide Headquarters

Reston, VA, USA		Darmstadt, Germany	
USA	Australia	Germany	Scandinavia
Canada	New Zealand	France	Austria
Central America	Japan	Spain	Switzerland
South America	Korea	Italy	Turkey
United Kingdom	Southeast Asia	Netherlands	Africa
Israel		Belgium	Middle East

NATURAL was the first end-user interactive database language and has since evolved into a premier production-oriented advanced application development environment.

SOFTWARE AG has continued to evolve and enhance a comprehensive set of tools and services that address all aspects of information processing. The company now provides more than 100 different products and services associated with application engineering, data management, and distributed computing.

As smaller, more powerful computers continue to flood the marketplace, migration paths for existing mission-critical mainframe-based applications are needed. SOFTWARE AG was one of the first companies to recognize this need and began development on its ENTIRE™ family of products in 1990.

Organizations moving to an open systems environment face the challenge of reconciling mainframe-based legacy systems with new technology. ENTIRE provides a smooth transition between the old and new worlds of computing, allowing companies to extend and evolve existing applications to newer and more cost-effective platforms—without sacrificing their software investment.

SOFTWARE AG recognized early in its history that the service and support provided with software products are as important as the products themselves. "We believe strongly that our success is very much dependent upon the satisfaction of our customers in effectively using our products," says Joseph J. Agro, executive vice president of SOFTWARE AG of North America. As a result, the company operates customer training and technical support centers throughout the world to ensure successful implementation and ongoing use of its

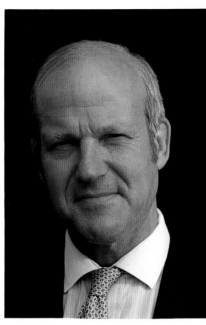

products.

The company's customer base represents virtually every industry group: agriculture and mining; manufacturing, transportation, and utilities; wholesale and retail; banking, finance, and insurance; business services, health care, and education; and state, local, federal, and foreign government.

With more than 4,000 employees supporting customers in over 62 countries and mangement duties spread across the two headquarters, "SOFTWARE AG still thinks of itself as a single entity, a single headquarters located in two cities," says Agro. Reston serves as the worldwide marketing headquarters, with R&D-oriented functions managed in Germany. SOFTWARE AG recently marked its 22nd consecutive profitable year with revenues reaching $470 million for 1991. This growth is a clear indication of the company's stability and longevity. An installed base of more than 5,000 satisfied customers offers testament to SOFTWARE AG's continued strength in the marketplace.

Left: Michael J. King, President and CEO of Software AG of North America, Inc.

Below: Broader Enterprise Computing Solution

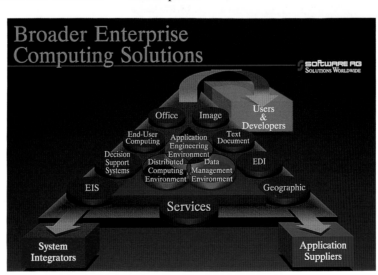

EDS

EDS (Electronic Data Systems) is a proud member of the Washington Metropolitan Area. The corporation, with over 70,000 employees in 30 countries, generated more than $7.1 billion in revenues in 1991. EDS opened its East Coast headquarters in Herndon, Virginia, in 1988. The facility, located on 202 acres near Dulles International Airport, features a 382,000-square-foot office building which houses a majority of the 3,000 Washington area employees. The Herndon employees support the Government Services Group which is responsible for the Military Systems Division, Government Services Division and the State Operations Division. The alignment of the government sectors emphasizes the sharing and application of EDS' information technology experience across government lines from the local to the

Below: EDS employs about 70,000 people worldwide—3,000 in the Washington Metropolitan Area. EDS' eastern regional headquarters is located in Herndon, Virginia

federal level. Groups serving EDS' commercial customers are also included in the Washington area.

The Herndon location also includes one of EDS' 18 Information Processing Centers (IPCs). These facilities form the backbone of the company's worldwide information processing and communications network—EDS*NET. The IPCs have enough on-line capacity to store a 600-word biography on every person in the world. The network is monitored and controlled through the Information Management Center in Plano, Texas.

With its corporate headquarters in Dallas, Texas, EDS is the world's leader in applying-information technology services, which include consulting, systems development,

Right: More than one millionstudenys across North America have participated in three Jason expeditions, sponsored by EDS and led by Dr. Robert Ballard. Photo by Maria Stenzel, National Geographic Society

systems integration, systems management, and communications. The company is organized in 38 strategic business units focusing on markets such as banking, insurance, energy, manufacturing, retailing, government, communications, pharmaceuticals, transportation, energy, and entertainment.

What does EDS do? EDS does not produce commercial software products, but its systems engineers write software programs and manage thousands of applications currently available to customers. Likewise, EDS is not a hardware manufacturer; however, it does make diverse hardware products work together.

In order to fulfill the requirements of more than 7,000 customers worldwide, EDS evaluates hardware, software, and networking products of more than 6,000 technology vendors. Its engineers make dissimilar technologies work together to accomplish specific customer goals while providing training to users and systems maintenance.

The company's allegiance is to the customer's quest for success. EDS chooses and applies the technology which best suits the needs of its customers.

The driving force behind the State Operations Division is to help customers manage change and respond to the complex challenges of the future. EDS acccomplishes this by partnering with state and local agencies across all types of public service by sharing information and maximizing limited resources and revenues.

Federal budget restraints present great challenges for agencies, both military and civilian, to maintain performance capabilities. The Federal business provides information technology services that emphasize the value of efficient and responsible state-of-the-art integrated systems.

COMMUNITY RELATIONS

EDS is also involved in numerous projects which enhance the communities where EDS employees live and work. These include the JASON Project, Vietnam Veterans *In Touch* program, the Smithsonian Institution's Information Age Exhibit, and EDS' Education Outreach Program.

The JASON Foundation for Education

The JASON Foundation encourages the study of science and technology among students. Started by Dr. Robert Ballard of Woods Hole Oceanographic Institution, it is strongly supported by EDS. Each year, thousands of North American students participate in an electronic field trip to some of the world's most fascinating places. The JASON Project uses cutting-edge technology and a hands-on approach to learning.

JASON Jr., a 200-pound, deep-sea robotic vehicle, attracted national attention with its discoveries of the *Titanic* and the *Bismarck*. The first televised JASON expedition, held in 1989, ventured to the Mediterranean Sea to explore the site of an ancient Roman shipwreck. In 1990 JASON journeyed to the underwater graves of the U.S. warships *Hamilton* and *Scourge* which were sunk during the War of 1812. Over half a million students watched in 20 downlink sites and closed television stations, as JASON explored the Galapagos Islands in 1991. One of the downlink sites is the National Geographic Society's Grosvenor Auditorium in Washington, D.C. JASON will continue in 1993 to the Sea of Cortez.

The JASON Project marks the world's first venture into the broadcast of live color images from actual sites of scientific discovery. Called "telepresence," this live adventure provides viewers an extraordinary you-are-there experience.

In Touch

The *In Touch* Program is a free nationwide locator service that helps veterans, families, and friends of those lost in Vietnam find each other. The technology supporting the *In Touch* program provides a lifeline to those who lost a loved one in the Southeast Asian conflict.

EDS developed and donated the information system to the Friends of the Vietnam Veterans Memorial, a non-profit organization in the Washington, D.C., area. The heart of

the system is a data base that contains the names of the 58,183 men and women listed on the National Vietnam Veterans Memorial "Wall" as well as information on friends, families, and comrades.

Since the system was first introduced on Memorial Day 1990, EDS has managed the system and provided volunteer support. More than 2,000 EDS employees in cities throughout the U.S. have volunteered to demonstrate the system, distribute *In Touch* data forms, and enter the data collected into the system.

EDS, with its more than 2,000 EDS Vietnam veterans, shows its respect and admiration for the men and women who died in Vietnam by donating this gift. *In Touch* will continue to extend the healing legacy of the National Vietnam Veterans Memorial.

Smithsonian's Information Age: People, Information and Technology

In 1990 the Smithsonian Institution's National Museum of American History opened an exhibit capturing the 150 years of information technology progression. Entitled *Information Age: People, Information and Technology,* the exhibit guides visitors

The EDS Information Management Center (IMC) demonstrates EDS' commitment to providing state-of-the-art systems management to customers by using the best in information technology. From the IMC, specialists coordinate the operations of 18 IPCs worldwide.

For the Smithsonian Institution's

Information Age exhibition, EDS

combined diverse technologies—in-

cluding laser audio and video,

robotics, and interactive visitor

workstations—to guide visitors

through the progression of informa-

tion technology.

through the development of the telephone, radio, television, and computer and shows how they have led the world into an electronic information age.

EDS made the Smithsonian's exhibit a reality by integrating the technology provided by 24 different corporate sponsors into one cohesive network. Comprised of 62 computers, 44 video disc players, 32 video monitors, and 19 bar code readers, the network enables visitors to test their knowledge and participate in simulated situations through the use of computer stations.

As visitors journey through the 14,000-square-foot area and explore the various "interactives" (two-way electronic communication systems), the network collects and records their personal experiences into a database. A record recapping an individual's activities in the exhibition is printed for each visitor.

The Smithsonian exhibit is both artistic and humanistic in its proof that art and technology can not only co-exist, but are logical companions. It will run until the year 2000.

Education Outreach

EDS has declared education as its number one community priority and has launched a multi-faceted program called Education Outreach. The goal is to improve the quality of education by working with students to positively effect the learning process. Local institutions with which EDS has formed partnerships include Floris Elementary School, John Adams Elementary School, Roper Junior High School, Scott Montgomery Elementary School, Herndon High School, and South Lakes High School. An EDS official

serves on the Fairfax County Public Schools Education Foundation as a board member.

EDS also encourages learning outside of the classroom for students and faculty. Employee volunteer mentor programs show the benefits of staying in school and offer children positive role models. In addition, EDS lends support to the Summer Institute of the Business Institute for Educators (BIE), a partnership of businesses and educators working to promote ties between schools and corporations. The Summer Institute offers two-week summer sessions that give nearly 300 educators and administrators a first-hand view of the corporate environment.

Volunteer Projects, Charitable Contributions, and Associations

Hundreds of EDS employees and their families volunteer their support for numerous area projects. These programs address various aspects of community life: cultural, recreational, environmental, and civic. EDS and 50 area companies were able to raise over $173,000 for Junior Achievement during the 1992 "Bowl for Business." Other worthwhile causes included the March of Dimes WalkAmerica, Adopt-A-Highway, Special Olympics, the International Children's Festival, holiday food and toy drives, and the Patriot's Cup Challenge, an annual 8K race held to benefit the Association of Retarded Citizens.

Another way in which the company helps the community is through charitable contributions. "Your gift touches home" best describes the need to support the 230 agencies within Fairfax County alone that rely upon the United Way. By becoming a donor, businesses ensure that needed human services will be available to solve personal problems as they arise. Through EDS' employee support, almost $300,000 has been raised for the Fairfax/Falls Church United Way Campaign over the past two years. Other contributions made include local police and fire departments, WETA, AAUW (American Association of University Women), and the Women's Center of Northern Virginia.

Leadership in the communities is as important as volunteerism and contributions. EDS executives serve on the boards of Junior Achievement, United Way, Make-A-Wish Foundation of Greater Washington, Wolf Trap, and the Fairfax County Chamber of Commerce.

The company is also represented in business associations. EDS employees currently

Left: For the Friends of the Vietnam Veteran's Memorial, EDS developed and donated an information system that links together families and friends of those lost in the conflict. EDS volunteers attend veteran's events nationwide distributing *In Touch* brochures and assisting those still healing from the effects of the Vietnam War.

rently hold board positions in the Armed Forces Communications and Electronics Association, ITAA, the Association of the United States Army, the Navy League, the Fairfax County Chamber of Commerce, the Air Force Association, the National Electrical Manufacturers Association, the American Public Welfare Association, and the Dulles Area Transportation Association (DATA).

While EDS' business is information technology services, it has extended its vision far beyond typical or traditional corporate boundaries. EDS is combining the skills and talents of its people with other corporate resources and applying this powerful integrated system for the support of the larger community.

Below: EDS supports a wide range of civic, charitable and cultural endeavors. Here, more than 150 EDS employees gather at the base of the Washington Monument to participate in a 15-mile walk in support of the March of Dimes' WalkAmerica program.

Systems Center, Inc., of Reston, Virginia, is a leading developer and marketer of systems and network management software. The company's products assist in the automation and control of mixed computing environments, enabling businesses worldwide to obtain maximum performance from their human and technological resources.

The company was founded in 1981 by Robert E. Cook. The company now sells a wide range of software products that provide its customers with the solutions they need to productively use and manage their systems and networks to meet the business goals of their enterprises.

Systems Center maintained a high profit margin and a steady growth rate throughout the 1980s. From a base of $2 million in 1982, Systems Center's annual revenues rose to $21 million in 1985, to $78 million in 1989, and passed $123 million in 1991. Systems Center stock has been traded on the New York Exchange since 1988. That kind of performance attracts major media attention. *Business Week* and *Forbes* both identified Systems Center as one of the nation's top growth firms of the 1980s.

Systems Center has evolved along with the needs of the industry it serves. In the early 1980s the company helped mainframe data processing managers maintain standardization and control. Today, complex networks and systems require sophisticated tools to manage the commands, messages, and responses generated by the flow of data across the information systems of the business enterprise. Systems Center, with its founding principle of anticipating and expanding into emerging high-growth markets, developed its products over the past 10 years to meet these changing requirements.

Robert E. Cook, chairman and chief executive officer of Systems Center, Inc.

In 1989 Systems Center acquired Australia's Software Developments International, owner and developer of Advanced Systems Management products. The Advanced Systems Management products provide an integrated environment to manage computer networks and achieve systems automation. The products feature an Expert System Foundation that automatically "learns" message flows and responses, and creates rules from predefined templates using high-level computer language support. The network operator is thus free to perform other tasks.

In addition, Systems Center obtained worldwide marketing rights to the product from Cincom Systems, Inc. The acquisition of the Advanced Systems Management products, considered the most advanced network management software on the market, has enabled Systems Center to form strategic al-

liances with AT&T, Digital Equipment Corporation, Tandem Computers, Hitachi, and Fujitsu, among others, to serve as additional distribution channels for the product.

This positions Systems Center as one of the top independent systems and network software companies. Systems Center products are sold in 60 countries and used by many of the world's largest organizations. According to Cook, "We've always been an independent software company. Today we're something more: a neutral player that can help customers manage information resources from many different vendors without compromising their choices."

Another major product area, Network DataMover® (NDM®), involves the automation of data transfer and related processing activities. In 1988 Systems Center acquired the marketer of NDM, The Systems Center, Inc., of Dallas, Texas. As this acquisition

marked the company's first venture into the networking market, the company changed its name from VM Software to Systems Center, Inc., to reflect its new focus. Systems Center's NDM product line has become a standard for automated data transfer in the securities, banking, insurance, and health care industries. NDM increases the speed, accuracy, and performance of file transfer across a variety of computer platforms.

Systems Center is an active member of the greater Washington community. The company has been deeply involved with regional education. Cook is a member of the board of trustees of the Fairfax County Public Schools Education Foundation, and Systems Center was instrumental in funding the library at Fairfax County's Thomas Jefferson High School for Science and Technology. The high school for gifted students serves much of Northern Virginia.

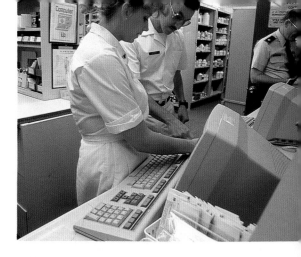

SAIC

Science Applications International Corporation (SAIC) was founded in 1969 by Dr. J. Robert Beyster and a small group of research scientists in La Jolla, California. SAIC is now America's largest employee-owned research and development company. The firm's 1991 sales exceeded $1.2 billion. It achieved a compound growth rate of above 20 percent per year for 20 years.

A diversified high-technology company, SAIC has more than 14,000 employees in over 300 offices worldwide.

Focused principally in the areas of national security, energy, the environment, health, and transportation, SAIC's business involves the application of scientific and engineering expertise—together with computer and systems technology—to solve complex technical problems. Since its formation, SAIC has been committed to making significant contributions to both public- and private-sector programs.

From developing and applying advanced technology to providing technical and management services, SAIC plays a major role in programs designed to strengthen the national security and industrial competitiveness of America and its allies.

SAIC constantly faces new technological challenges in the development and analysis of advanced military systems and strategies. In the national security arena, SAIC performs a wide range of activities for the Department

of Defense, the Department of Energy, and other agencies.

SAIC's energy-related activities involve work for a wide range of government and commercial customers. They include projects in such areas as safety evaluations, security, reliability and availability, engineering evaluations, technical reviews, quality assurance, information systems, plant-monitoring systems, instrumentation and control systems, and project management.

SAIC is a major provider of technology to the nuclear utility industry, as well as a supplier of fuel cell, alternative energy, and coal and oil analysis technology. The company develops probabilistic risk assessments for nuclear utilities and provides engineering and analytical support to major fusion laboratories.

SAIC has expanded its support efforts in the siting of an underground repository for high-level nuclear wastes, performing analyses ranging from geologic site characterization to environmental assessment.

SAIC also applies its multidisciplinary expertise to a broad range of programs designed to provide better health care and improved conditions in the work place and the environment. Among the skills SAIC brings to bear on important environmental problems are hazardous waste management, remedial action investigations, water-quality programs, and dredged material dispersal.

SAIC investigators played a major role in assessing the damage to Prince William Sound in the aftermath of the 1989 Alaskan oil spill.

In 1990 SAIC helped design and install a Proton Beam Therapy System for the Loma Linda University Medical Center.

In 1991 SAIC won a contract to manage a new program for the U.S. Army for chemical demilitarization. SAIC is supplying the Army with a broad range of technological, environmental, integration, and program planning support.

SAIC is also involved with a $1.1-billion contract with the Department of Defense to install a computer-based medical information system in military hospitals and clinics around the world. When completed, the Composite Health Care System will significantly improve the military's ability to manage and access enormous quantities of medical data.

SAIC grew rapidly throughout the 1980s. The company projects continued growth rates in excess of 10 percent per year. SAIC intends to apply its energy and talent to improve the productivity of governmental organizations and increase the competitiveness of industry.

SAIC is no stranger to competition. In 1987 the firm was the key technical support contractor for the design and technology team that designed *Stars and Stripes* for the America's Cup competition. The group's efforts contributed to major improvements in hull and keel design, as well as in performance evaluation technology.

Dr. Beyster, SAIC's founder, chief executive officer, and chairman of the board, believes that the company's success is largely due to its employee ownership system. The SAIC philosophy: "Those who contribute to the company should own it. Ownership should be proportional to that contribution and performance as much as feasible."

In 1986 Dr. Beyster established the Foundation for Enterprise Development, a nonprofit organization whose primary mission is to accelerate the adoption of employee ownership and involvement in U.S. companies. Dr. Beyster believes employee ownership and participation are crucial tools to improve U.S. competitiveness in world markets. The foundation sponsors seminars and other programs to assist businesses in adopting practical approaches to employee ownership.

SAIC has its national headquarters in San Diego, California. Its second-largest concentration of offices is in the Washington, D.C., region. SAIC has more than 3,000 employees in the national capital area.

Regional offices are located in McLean, Alexandria, Skyline City, Crystal City, Falls Church, Vienna, Arlington, and Reston, Virginia. Maryland locations include Germantown, Joppatowne, and Columbia.

SAIC's board of directors, chaired by Dr. Beyster, is composed of 22 senior executives from the firm and former high-level officials from industry and government. Dr. Larry Kull is president and chief operating officer. The company has four vice chairmen of the board: David Heebner, John McRary, Vince Cook, and William Zisch.

SAIC's team of highly talented professionals has built a reputation for solving complex technical systems integration and engineering problems through the application of advancing technologies. The SAIC philosophy of employee ownership and participation accounts for a large measure of its success. At SAIC, every aspect of the staff's diverse capabilities reflects its individual and collective commitment to technical excellence.

SAIC is strongly committed to being an active and effective corporate citizen in the Washington, D.C., metropolitan area. The company and its employees support many regional educational, health, and community services organizations. At SAIC, community service is seen as the logical extension of a corporate philosophy that is keyed to problem solving.

Above: For the America's Cup in 1987, *Stars and Stripes* was outfitted with an SAIC spinnaker.

Left: Following the 1989 Alaskan oil spill in Prince William Sound, SAIC investigators played a major role in assessing the damage.

IBM

Ninety-five years ago, the forerunner of what is today the world's largest computer company opened its doors in a square brick building along the old Chesapeake and Ohio canal. The company was called the Tabulating Machine Company. It was founded by Herman Hollerith, inventor of the first punched card tabulating machine. Hollerith and his inventions revolutionized data collection and heralded the start of the Information Age.

When Hollerith sold his business in 1911, the facility in the Georgetown section of Washington, D.C., became part of the newly formed Computing-Tabulating-Recording Company. Three years later Thomas J. Watson, Sr., joined the fledgling operation as general manager, and in 1924 the company changed its name to the International Business Machines Corporation.

Today IBM operates several major facilities in the Washington Metropolitan Area, including a manufacturing and development site in Manassas, Virginia, a federal sector marketing division in Bethesda, Maryland, and a regional commercial marketing headquarters in downtown Washington. Branch offices dot the local landscape. The company's more than 12,000 D.C.-area employees provide customers with advanced information technology designed to help meet the needs of large and small businesses, governmental agencies and educational institutions.

IBM's skilled work force develops, markets, installs, and maintains information processing systems, software, and related products that are tailored to customers' specific business requirements and provides information systems consulting services. IBM employees and IBM Business Partners, such as authorized dealers and re-marketers, mar-

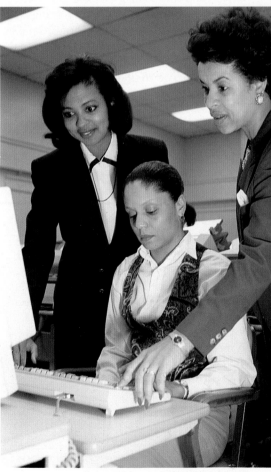

ket these offerings.

"Our product is solutions," says Greg Corgan, general manager of IBM's Washington Metropolitan Trading Area.

"We're here to solve our customers' problems, from the needs of a single user to the

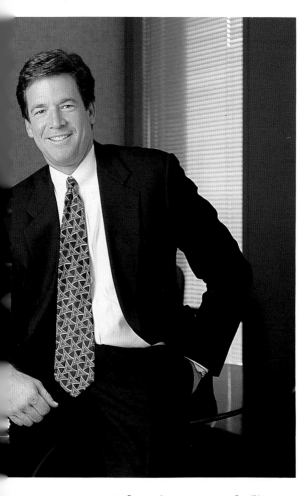

In 1991, the most recent year for which statistics are available, the IBM corporation and its employees committed almost $4 million to local United Way agencies and other local charities, and $150,000 in equipment to the Washington, D.C., school system.

Almost half of the IBM employees in this way volunteer their time to local charitable organizations. They work with "border babies," struggling young people, the homeless, and others in need.

IBM also donates its products and its employees' time to provide free job training for people unable to afford commercially available programs. IBM equipment and software grants totalling $300,000 during 1991 helped the Washington Urban League, Inc., and the Opportunities Industrialization Center (OIC) run two job training centers in this area. Together, those centers graduated 200 people and placed 90 percent of them in jobs.

Left: Greg Corgan, general manager, Washington Metropolitan Trading Area.

Below: IBM offers education and support to Washington Metropolitan Area customers through its Customer Center at 1301 K. Street, N.W.

management of a major corporate facility. Our people start an assignment by learning to understand their customers' businesses. They see themselves as partners with their customers, working together to achieve shared goals and objectives."

The IBM of the 1990s does everything from help customers identify ways information technology can make them more competitive to operating data processing facilities for them. This updated approach reflects an IBM that has at its core a truly customer-oriented view. The strategy has prompted IBM to engage increasingly in joint ventures and cooperative agreements with other members of the information technology industry.

Customer satisfaction is also the reason IBM has subdivided its regional business units (called areas) into "trading areas." Through the trading areas, IBM has placed more decision-making power and more easily shared skills closer to its customers. This enables the company to be more responsive to its customers needs.

The Washington Metropolitan Trading Area is one of eight that constitute the IBM Mid-Atlantic Area, which is headquartered in Washington, D.C., and guided by vice president and general manager Kenneth R. Thornton.

With both a trading area office and an area office based here, IBM feels an especially strong commitment to this community. That commitment is demonstrated not only by the company's business investment in the region, but also by its investment in the lives of Washington-area citizens.

In its Corporate Support Programs, such as those mentioned above, and in its daily business operations, IBM strives to be a company that first and foremost stands for quality. Says Corgan, "While our products and our methods for delivering them have changed dramatically from the days of Herman Hollerith and Tom Watson, Sr., the basic principles that Watson established for the company haven't changed at all. We still believe in respect for the individual, service to the customer and excellence—read quality—in everything we do."

QUALITY OF LIFE

Enjoying the Region's Offerings

Education and medical institutions, as well as hotels, retail establishments, and service industries, help shape and improve the lives of capital region residents.

Photo by Michael Ventura/Folio

MARYMOUNT UNIVERSITY

Above: Marymount's historic Main House graces the front of the university's campus in residential Arlington, Virginia. The university also offers courses at other sites in Northern Virginia.

Below: A low student-faculty ratio offers excellent opportunities for interaction between Marymount's well-qualified faculty and 3,300 undergraduate and graduate students. Pictured, Dr. Wayne Lesko, professor of psychology, discusses his field with students between classes. Photo by James Cohrssen

The graceful, bucolic calm of Marymount University's Northern Virginia campus makes it easy to forget that it is located just a few minutes' drive from the White House and the Library of Congress.

The traditions at Marymount date back to the nineteenth-century roots of the French Religious of the Sacred Heart of Mary order whose philosophy led to the creation of this institution. But the curriculum, methodology, and technological support are appropriate to a university preparing students for the coming century.

Marymount was founded in 1950 as a two-year women's college. In 1973 it became a four-year college offering bachelor's degrees in more than 20 different academic disciplines. In 1979 the college added coeducational graduate programs.

The institution became fully coeducational in 1986, simultaneously adding a satellite campus and changing its name to Marymount University. Since then the University has continued expanding, growing both in the numbers of students it serves and in the diversity of its academic offerings.

Marymount University today, which has more than 3,300 students enrolled at both the undergraduate and graduate levels, is an independent institution related to the Catholic Church and governed by a fully autonomous board of trustees. The board includes leaders in both the national and local business communities, alumni, and members of the Religious of the Sacred Heart of Mary.

Despite its rapid growth, Marymount has maintained its commitment to value-centered education and to a campus atmosphere in which students have an awareness of ethical values and a concern for others. In addition, the development of students as mature individuals remains a priority for Marymount faculty and administrators.

"We're the University that cares," says Sister M. Majella Berg, RHSM, president. "We care, but we don't coddle. Marymount students learn to appreciate their own potential, and they learn to work for it."

Marymount prepares its students for modern life by providing specialized studies within the context of a well-rounded, liberal arts education. The University offers more than 40 majors in four schools: Arts and Sciences, Business Administration, Education and Human Services, and Nursing. In preparation for a career, all Marymount undergraduates complete a senior-year internship,

with the resources of the nation's capital providing unparalleled opportunities in business, government, communications, education, and health care.

In the School of Arts and Sciences, the University's Clare Boothe Luce Endowment supports distinguished professors in mathematics, computer science, and biology. The Luce Endowment also funds scholarships to outstanding undergraduate women interested in mathematics or science careers. Marymount's interior design, fashion design, and merchandising programs continue to receive extensive national recognition.

Nursing was the first professional curriculum offered at Marymount, and its graduates have been actively recruited by regional hospitals since 1968. Marymount's Education graduates are also well respected in the community, with the school's innovative programs widely studied and imitated by other academic institutions. And Marymount's School of Business, widely acclaimed for its MBA program, cooperates with area corporations for the benefit of both student and business.

Student life at Marymount is rich with activities, including a Campus Ministry that continues to play a guiding role and provide for spiritual growth through daily Mass and other interdenominational religious programs and community service projects.

Marymount's athletics programs, which compete at the NCAA Division III level, have expanded rapidly since the University became coed. The department now boasts five women's and six men's teams, and the basketball programs have consistently improved to become two of the region's finest.

The University's 18-acre main campus is located in a residential neighborhood of north Arlington County, with 600 undergraduates living in on-campus residence halls. The nearby Spout Run satellite campus houses the academic computer center as well as classroom space. The University operates additional off-campus facilities at Ballston, in Loudoun County, the Pentagon, and at corporate sites throughout Northern Virginia. Marymount's shuttle bus system, with service to two Metro subway stations, enables students to take advantage of Washington's cultural and educational opportunities.

As the next century approaches, Marymount University will maintain its commitment to quality education and continue to evolve to fulfill the changing needs of the greater Washington, D.C., community.

DESIGN CUISINE

In Washington, D.C.'s high-profile social scene, savvy event planners rely on Design Cuisine and its subsidiary, DC Rental, to set a magnificent table with exciting food. In fact, Design Cuisine has set tables for the Queen of England and many heads of state. And when Hollywood comes to Washington to premier movies such as *Dick Tracy* and *Batman Returns*, it is usually Design Cuisine that provides the creative menu, while DC Rental sets the special table that echos the film's motif.

The success of Design Cuisine and DC Rental stems from years of experience. Founded in 1982 by William Homan, Horst Klein, and Steve Veletsis, Design Cuisine grew from their common belief that every special event requires reliable service, innovative menus, flexible planning, and attention to detail. The trio developed this approach to catering while operating their first joint venture, a popular D.C. restaurant.

Putting theory into practice, Design Cuisine earned a reputation for consistent high quality food and service. In 1983 it catered an event hosted by President and Mrs. Reagan to honor the late princess Grace and Monaco's royal family. Since then the organization has created exceptional luncheons, receptions, and dinners for dignitaries and celebrities from around the world.

Through responsive, individualized service, Homan, Klein, and Veletsis have pleased not only their guests of honor, but also Washington's most discriminating hosts. The key to the organization's success? "Flexibility—in responding to our clients' needs and in our signature approach to menu design, food preparation, and table settings," says Horst Klein.

The ability to accommodate a client's every need is the core of the Design Cuisine and DC Rental service concept. DC Rental creates totally customized events, providing tables, chairs, linens, china, and silverware. Even its standard supplies are available in a vast array of colors and styles. The most popular wood reception chair comes in eight finishes with more than thirty cushion designs.

The hallmark of DC Rental's service is its selection of table linens. Knowing that beautiful table settings enhance delicious meals, Homan, Klein, and Veletsis have created hundreds of choices from an international selection of designer fabrics. The company cuts and sews all of its linens in house and finishes them with select touches such as welting and fringes. This superb linen library includes im-

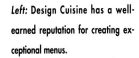

Left: Design Cuisine has a well-earned reputation for creating exceptional menus.

Below: DC Rental creates totally customized events, providing tables, chairs, linens, china, and silverware.

ported silks, Fortuni-like fabrics, tapestries, brocades, Battenberg lace, and Irish linen.

"The demand for these exquisite linens is enormous. We ship them all over the country," notes DC Rental sales manager Peter Grazzini. "We've even shipped linens to England, France, Italy, and Russia."

In addition to supplying all of the linens, furnishings, table settings, and other equipment used by Design Cuisine, DC Rental also rents its materials to hotels, corporations, florists, and other caterers needing a customized look.

"Every piece of equipment and furniture and each table linen returned to DC Rental's warehouse is cleaned, polished, and restored to mint condition," says Steve Veletsis.

In its self-sufficient way, the company maintains a laundry and paint and carpentry shop on its premises.

Design Cuisine and DC Rental operate from a multi-building complex near the Shirlington Gateway neighborhood of Arlington, Virginia, just off Interstate 395. Says Homan, "Our primary market is metropolitan Washington where we cater hundreds of events each year. But we've also catered spectacular gatherings in New York, Palm Beach, Boston, Chicago, and Nantucket. We are available to help create grand events anywhere in the world."

WASHINGTON ADVENTIST HOSPITAL

Right: The hospital's Special Additions Maternity Center emphasizes family-centered care in a home-like environment.

Below: Founded in 1907 in Takoma Park, Maryland, Washington Adventist Hospital is Montgomery County's longest-operating hospital.

Washington Adventist Hospital has a long history of service to residents of Washington, D.C., and the surrounding area. Since its beginnings in 1907, the hospital has grown to become a full-service, 300-bed hospital and Montgomery County's only complete cardiac care center. Washington Adventist performs 800 cardiac surgeries a year, and nearly 4,000 heart catheterizations and angioplasties. It was the first hospital in the Washington area to perform mitral valvuloplasty and the first non-teaching hospital in Maryland to perform ventricular ablation and directed coronary atherectomy. Washington Adventist also operates a Cardiac Rehabilitation Center and participates in FDA-approved clinical drug research.

More than 2,000 babies are born at the hospital's Special Additions Maternity Center each year. Washington Adventist emphasizes family-centered care in a homelike environment—offering eight labor-delivery-recovery (birthing) rooms. A Level II Nursery provides care for premature and sick babies and the hospital maintains a liberal visitor policy for family members. Parents can review their birthing choices at parent educa-

tion classes, and if the family so desires, siblings and grandparents may be present during deliveries.

The hospital's Radiation-Oncology Department is the only non-government, in-hospital facility in suburban Maryland to provide

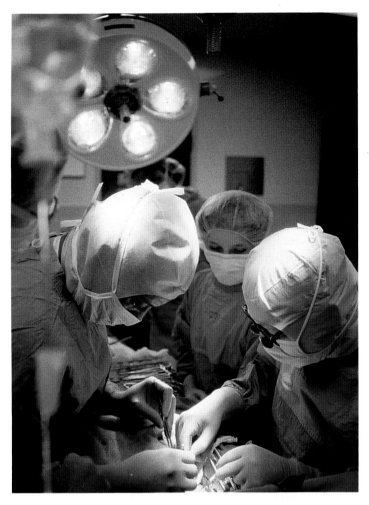

specialized care for cancer patients. Three treatment units with 10 different energies afford both physicians and patients the widest possible range of choices. The hospital's Siemens KD—a high-energy dual x-ray accelerator—was one of the first installed on the East Coast.

With 11 operating rooms and a short stay unit, Washington Adventist's Surgery Department handles more than 10,000 procedures each year, including cardiac, oncologic, ophthalmologic, and arthroscopic surgery. Using state-of-the-art equipment including lasers, surgeons perform new laparoscopic procedures that offer minimal scarring, increased patient comfort, quicker recovery, and shorter hospital stays.

The hospital's mental health center provides a full range of inpatient and outpatient programs for patients experiencing psychiatric difficulties, disabling anxieties, schizophrenia, or alcohol-related problems.

In addition to its discharge planning services, the highly respected Social Work/ Discharge Planning Department offers counseling to help patients make the emotional adjustment to illness. All staff members are trained at the master's level and are dedi-

cated to providing high-quality service to patients and their families. The Pastoral Care Department also helps meet patient and family needs throughout hospital stays. Chapel services are held daily and a chaplain is always on call.

Washington Adventist Hospital combines advanced technology with timeless compassion to provide the best in medical care. Since its 1907 origins, the hospital has also focused special attention on preventive medicine, proclaiming the virtues of exercise and sound nutrition long before they became a national trend.

Washington Adventist carries this health message to the community by offering regular classes on exercise, diet, smoking cessation, weight loss, and CPR certification, as well as health screenings that include cholesterol testing and nutrition counseling. The hospital's Lifeline program provides seriously ill or elderly patients with a personal emergency response system.

The hospital is a major employer in the community. Its staff members are active in many local and regional civic associations. In return, the community has contributed to the hospital. Its board of directors has included the mayor of Takoma Park, a state senator, and a past president of the Montgomery County Bar Association.

Washington Adventist Hospital is part of Adventist HealthCare Mid-Atlantic, a regional network that includes 11 not-for-profit health care organizations.

Left: Washington Adventist Hospital is renowned for its pioneering work in surgery and cardiology. As the only complete cardiac care center in five Maryland counties, Washington Adventist performs more than 800 cardiac surgeries each year.

Below left: The emergency department is an important component of any full-service hospital. Physicians and nurses at Washington Adventist Hospital deliver expert medical care 24 hours a day.

WASHINGTON, D.C. CONVENTION & VISITORS ASSOCIATION

Washington, D.C., is more than the political capital of the world. It is also the capital of the world of tourism and the world of trade associations. One local group ties all of these worlds together. The Washington, D.C. Convention & Visitors Association (WCVA) is a nonprofit organization established by the Washington region's community and business leaders to promote convention and pleasure travel to the greater Washington area.

"We have a world's fair between the Capitol and the Lincoln Memorial," says Daniel E. Mobley, CAE, executive vice president of WCVA. "It runs all day, every day of the year, and all of the major attractions are free. And beyond the monuments, Washington is a fascinating, complex city comprised of distinctive neighborhoods such as Georgetown, Adams-

A typical Adams Morgan neighborhood scene.

Morgan, and many others."

If you are thinking about visiting the District of Columbia, writing about Washington, leading a tour group to the nation's capital, or hosting a convention in the area, the association will be happy to provide assistance.

Prospective visitors receive maps and booklets telling all about the region and its hotels, attractions, and events. The package makes an informative and attractive introduction to Washington.

Inquiring reporters and writers receive stacks of fresh and timely press releases. The press materials cover everything that is happening in Washington from the Antiques Show in early January to the Christmas Pageant of Peace celebration in late December.

Professionals planning conventions and selling Washington as a travel destination receive a current "Destination Planning Kit" which includes a comprehensive directory of attractions, facilities, and tour services. Meeting and convention planners receive extensive literature and follow-up calls offering additional support and appropriate personalized assistance.

In 1990 WCVA responded to more than 200,000 requests for information about travel to the Washington, D.C., area. In response to growing international interest in Washington, the association has opened offices in Tokyo, London, and Frankfurt.

"International visitors have longer vacations than are typical for Americans," notes Mobley. "They spend weeks exploring our region, what we call 'George Washington country,' from the beach to the mountains. They spend much of that time in metropolitan Washington.

"Washington is the most popular tourist destination in the United States," says Mobley. "The Smithsonian's Air and Space Museum is the most visited museum in the world."

As travel and communications professionals throughout America have learned, WCVA provides outstanding service. Now that WCVA is expanding its efforts in the international arena, communications media personnel, tourists, and travel agents around the world

"family" destination, Washington leads the nation in "double-occupancy" convention bookings.)

They spent about $3.7 billion while they were here, generating tax revenues of $516 million.

They directly support approximately 40,000 hospitality industry jobs and indirectly support another 25,000-30,000 jobs.

"Washington's tourism industry is a critical link in developing a new base for our city's future economic vitality," says Sharon Pratt Kelly, mayor of the District of Columbia. "I am especially excited about WCVA's increased international marketing programs that promise to expand our share of the lucrative international tourism business."

In addition to responding to requests for assistance, WCVA represents the region at domestic and international trade shows, initiates sales calls, hosts educational tours for travel agents and tour planners, and produces a variety of marketing support materials

The association's public relation campaign, an essential element of its overall marketing efforts, annually generates millions of dollars worth of travel publicity about Washington. WCVA staff are often intimately involved in the publication of exciting travel articles. In recent years, the association has hosted a series of special tours for visiting travel writers from around the world, and provided support to thousands of other writers and editors.

In addition to its outreach activities, WCVA operates the Washington Visitors Information Center at 1455 Pennsylvania Ave., NW. The center is a walk-in tourist facility, a "one-stop-shopping" resource for free brochures, maps, and personal advice on visiting the nation's capital. The center is open six days a week throughout the year. It is staffed by WCVA staff and by trained volunteers.

Mobley has been WCVA executive vice president since 1990. William Edwards, general manager of the Washington Hilton and Towers, is president of WCVA. Sheila Stampfli, executive vice president of Courtesy Associates, is first vice president.

will also be learning about this extraordinary regional resource.

Founded in 1931, WCVA and its members represent every segment of the Washington hospitality industry. Subscribing companies include most of the area's leading hotels, restaurants, attractions, retailers, theaters, transportation companies, travel and tour service providers, convention suppliers, and other groups.

The association is supported by the voluntary annual dues of these subscribers, and by an appropriation from the District of Columbia government—a contribution based on the hotel tax receipts.

Tourism remains the second-largest industry in the area, exceeded in its financial importance to the region only by the federal government.

In 1990, approximately 19 million visitors came to Washington.

To house them, the metropolitan area provides more than 68,000 hotel rooms. (As a

FAIRFAX HOSPITAL

The national capital region hosts a rich collection of medical institutions. None is more admired by the profession or appreciated by its community than Fairfax Hospital. Fairfax Hospital opened as a small community hospital 31 years ago. Since then it has become a 656-bed regional medical center.

Independent consumer research studies routinely reflect the high regard regional residents have for Fairfax Hospital. Fairfax is the hospital most often identified as providing the "best overall quality" and as "having the best image and reputation."

Fairfax Hospital's reputation for quality care has attracted more than 1,500 physicians to its medical staff. These community-based physicians are deeply involved in the development of patient care programs, medical quality assurance programs, and long-term planning for the hospital. Fairfax also provides clinical experience for interns and residents from the medical schools at Georgetown and George Washington universities and the Medical College of Virginia.

The nursing staff at Fairfax Hospital is equally exceptional, with 1,600 dedicated nursing professionals working in medical specialties ranging from pediatrics and obstetrics to trauma and critical care. Fairfax is affiliated with nursing programs at George Mason University, Marymount University, and Northern Virginia Community College.

Medical, Surgical, and Critical Care: Fairfax Hospital believes that its medical, surgical, and critical care services form the core of its operations. The medical, surgical, and critical care teams recognize that health problems are rarely subject to simple

compartmentalization. The program brings together outstanding physicians and surgeons from a wide variety of specialties. At Fairfax Hospital, patients with multisystem problems receive treatment from a multidisciplinary health care team.

Cardiac Care: From medical care for heart attack patients to coronary artery bypass and heart and lung transplant surgery, the Virginia Heart Center at Fairfax Hospital provides Washington-area residents with world-class heart care. The region's first heart transplant was performed at Fairfax Hospital. As a national test site for new cardiac care treatments and technology, the Virginia Heart Center offers patients both the benefits of the latest medical innovations and the expertise of a renowned team of cardiovascular specialists.

Obstetrics and Gynecology: Over its 31-year history Fairfax Hospital has assisted the births of more than 170,000 babies. The hospital provides a widely respected high-risk obstetrics unit and testing center, and Northern Virginia's top-rated newborn intensive care unit.

In 1992 Fairfax Hospital opened its new Women and Children's Center, a seven-story, 300,000-square-foot facility designed to provide the region's newest and most advanced facilities for obstetrics, pediatrics, and gynecological care.

Pediatric Care: Medical science is increasingly aware of the unique needs of infants, children, and adolescents. At Fairfax Hospital, children with a wide variety of medical or surgical problems receive expert care from highly trained specialists. In Northern

Virginia's only pediatric intensive care unit, specialists work around the clock caring for young trauma victims, cardiac patients, and children with life-threatening illnesses.

Cancer Care: The Cancer Center at Fairfax Hospital is a center of hope. In conjunction with its community-based physician specialists, the center provides full diagnostic and treatment capabilities. It is Northern Virginia's only cancer center with a pediatric cancer specialist, and is accredited by the American College of Surgeons as a teaching hospital cancer program. To complement the center's outstanding medical treatment, its Life with Cancer program provides patients and their families with emotional and educational support.

Emergency and Trauma Care: Board-certified emergency physicians and pediatric emergency specialists, trauma surgeons, anesthesiologists, intensive care physicians, radiologists, and support staff in the laboratory, X-ray, and surgery departments are available around the clock to treat the most seriously ill and injured patients, as well as those patients with less serious conditions.

The trauma team treats the most critical cases, those requiring immediate and extensive medical intervention. The trauma unit is Northern Virginia's only Level I trauma center. The hospital's emergency medical helicopter, Inova Medical AirCare, is always available to emergency service professionals. It is used both to transport staff to accident scenes and patients to the hospital.

Supportive Services: Fairfax Hospital provides assistance to patients and their families throughout their stay—starting with help with the registration and financial procedures. Social workers, child life specialists, and creative arts therapists work with patients to help them deal with the emotional

aspects of trauma and illness. Hundreds of volunteers from throughout the Northern Virginia community, including chaplains from every major religious group, assist patients and their families throughout their stay.

Community Health Education: The HealthSource of Fairfax Hospital offers community education programs in heart health, children's health, maternity care, nutrition and fitness, health for seniors, cancer care, stress management, and many other areas. Fairfax Hospital also offers patients and their families health education on diabetes, stroke rehabilitation, cardiac catheterization, pediatric surgery, and other topics.

Fairfax Hospital is part of Inova Health Systems, a comprehensive, not-for-profit health care organization serving all of Northern Virginia. Other hospitals in the system include Fair Oaks, Jefferson, and Mount Vernon. Inova also provides a variety of extended and noncritical services, such as long-term care, home care, and addiction treatment.

Left: Fairfax Hospital offers Northern Virginia a complete range of specialized pediatric services to meet the unique medical needs of children.

Below: From its heart and lung transplant program to its comprehensive cardiac surgery capabilities, The Virginia Heart Center at Fairfax Hospital offers one of the region's finest cardiac care services.

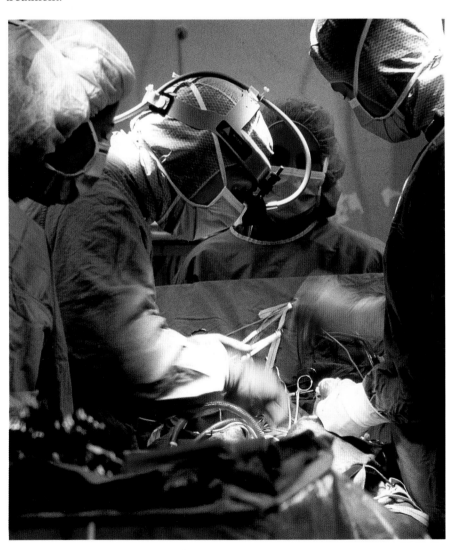

B & B WASHINGTON'S CATERER

When you are responsible for selecting a caterer for the Republican Party's Presidential Dinner, you can be as demanding and selective as you like. Of course the fans at RFK Stadium can be just as demanding and vociferous about their hot dogs and French fries.

What does the food at the Presidential Dinner have to do with a stadium hot dog? Both are the responsibility of Washington's premier purveyor to parties, B & B.

The hot dogs come from B & B Stadium Services. The Presidential Dinner is provided by B & B Washington's Caterer, the company's fine catering division. The other two B & B divisions are B & B Recreational Services, which caters company picnics and similar casual outdoor events, and Les Entrees, a gourmet take-out operation based in Potomac.

B & B is owned by the Birgfeld family, consisting of Mrs. Lola Mae Birgfeld and her two sons, H. William Birgfeld III, president and Robert A. Birgfeld, vice president, secretary, and treasurer. "We do it all," says Birgfeld. "We do fine catering for weddings and bar mitzvahs, international gourmet dinners for the embassies, hot dogs at the stadium, and beer and barbecued ribs for the Hot Rod Show at the National Guard Armory. We have a 40,000-square-foot warehouse. We can provide paper and plastic disposables or elegant imported crystal and sterling silver table service."

The B & B warehouse, commissary, and corporate offices can be found behind a plain, commercial exterior on the northern edge of the district. Inside, however, if a customer comes by to audition the service or taste-test a proposed menu, he or she may find a table set with Irish linen, French crystal, and English sterling silver. In the attached commercial kitchens an international staff that includes several of Washington's most distinguished chefs and a remarkably talented corps of assistants work its culinary magic.

"The world of food is changing around us," says Birgfeld. We used to have to go to Europe to recruit our chefs. Now, many of our finest people are raised and trained in Washington. But then the quality of Washington restaurants and the expectations of our customers have changed a lot, too. There are a lot of good ethnic restaurants around, now. Washington has learned to appreciate the foods from a lot of different cultures. We do the kitchens of the world from our commissary. We're Greek today, French tomorrow, Irish the next day, and Mexican the day after that."

All four divisions of B & B share a single commissary. On occasion, they work together. B & B Stadium Services is responsible for the cafeterias, concessions, and special events at the National Guard Armory and

This was the scene in the Statuary Hall of the nation's Capitol Building when B & B catered an event on behalf of President Lech Walesa of Poland where 175 dignitaries were invited to a formal seated dinner. Photo courtesy of Arnold Grant

RFK. But when the art dealers come to town, B & B Washington Caterers helps with the crepes and champagne. The fine catering division also takes complete responsibility for the more elaborate sports banquets.

"We have to be flexible and diversified," says Birgfeld. "That's what this city is all about. We serve a banquet to Friends of the Earth one day and cater a Paul McCartney concert or a corporate reception the next day." To meet such eclectic demand, everything at B & B is totally customized and nothing is prepackaged.

B & B has its own bakery, pastry shop, and other specialized facilities. The company even maintains a special stock of supplies used exclusively for kosher catering. (To be kosher, the food and everything associated with its preparation and serving must meet strict Jewish dietary laws.) B & B's "strictly kosher" assignments include not only bar mitzvah celebrations, but, on at least one memorable recent occasion, a formal State Department reception for Israeli leaders.

B & B has been catering inaugural balls since 1948 when Harry Truman was the guest of honor. It handled Washington Mayor Sharon Pratt Kelly's fancy dress party at Union Station and the tent party in Southeast D. C.

The company was started by H. William Birgfeld Jr. and his wife Lola Mae. After Mr. Birgfeld's death, H. William Birgfeld III took over the operation. B & B served its first meals during World War II and one of its initial operations was providing food service to troop trains passing through Washington, D.C. The company originally provided in-plant food services, with a marketing area stretching from New Haven, Connecticut, to Norfolk, Virginia. It provided food services at the Glen Echo amusement park until 1961.

The company's shift to fine catering came gradually, and it came at the public's request. "Corporate affairs became increasingly fancy. So did the Washington life-style," recalls Birgfeld. "As the times changed and Washington changed, B & B changed too.

"The development of Washington over the past 30 years has been unique. It's made us a unique company," says Birgfeld. "Most people who do sporting events can't do fine catering. Because of our history and our close relationship to the community, we've learned to do it all.

"We serve dinners at the embassies and refreshments at Jack Kent Cooke's box at

RFK. We've served dinners for 4 people and for 4,000. We've served at most of the embassies in town, at the Supreme Court, the Capitol, all of the art galleries, most of the law firms, and a lot of private homes."

B & B's recreational division is just as flexible and just as accommodating. The group hosts company picnics, association fund raisers, casual social affairs, and similar events. B & B will provide everything you need, from tables and utensils to games and entertainment. The food can be anything from hot dogs and hamburgers to a down-home pork barbecue, shrimp tempura, beef burritos (it once served a Mexican dinner in the U. S. Senate), chicken cacciatore, falafel, or a vegetarian Indian curry.

B & B's newest venture is Les Entrees, a full-meal gourmet carry-out operation based in Potomac. "Two-income families may not have time to cook, but they still want to enjoy gourmet cuisine," says Bergfeld. "That what Les Entrees is all about."

The Washington life-style is still changing. So B & B is still changing, too. But at B & B, you can be sure that anything it does will be in the best of taste.

This spectacular setting was arranged by the catering company for a formal dinner for 1,700 guests at the National Building Museum in Washington, D.C. The event honored all of the American Catholic cardinals and included dignitaries from the United States and around the world. Photo courtesy of Arnold Grant

THE PARK HYATT HOTEL

There is a grand piano in the presidential suite of Washington's Park Hyatt Hotel, along with an exquisite collection of antique oriental art and many other luxurious amenities. The suite is favored by the princess of Brunei and other royal guests, including members of the Saudi and Jordanian aristocracies.

For those whose requirements may be less sublime, the Park Hyatt offers 223 other spacious rooms and suites. For all of its guests, no matter which accommodations are selected, the Park Hyatt provides services and attention to detail that exceed international five-star standards.

Copies of *Le Monde, Frankfurter Allgemeine*, and *Al Ahram* await guests in the lobby of Washington's Park Hyatt Hotel every morning as a service for the hotel's multicultural international clientele. Located at 24th and M streets, the four-star luxury hotel is just a few minutes' stroll from Georgetown, the business district, and the historic West End neighborhoods.

The lobbies and public rooms of the Washington Park Hyatt reflect its high standards. The surroundings include original artwork by Calder, Picasso, and Matisse. Exquisite oriental antiques, an eclectic collection of oriental and American sculpture, and the creations of leading Washington artists illuminate the public areas.

Park Hyatt is a special division of Chicago-based Hyatt Hotels. Park Hyatt hotels are located in London, Sydney and Canberra, Tokyo, Beijing, and Madrid.

In the United States, Park Hyatt operates hotels in Chicago, New York (the U.N. Plaza Hotel), San Francisco, and Washington. In almost all of its markets, Park Hyatt has become the leading luxury hotel catering to the small convention and business market. It is among America's leading hosts of corporate directors and other core leadership groups.

No wonder: For today's high-tech communicators, all Park Hyatt rooms include multi-line telephones with computer hookups. Oversized bathtubs, superb soaps, and plush terry cloth robes await the sojourning sybarite. Every room also features a fully-stocked minibar, marble bathroom, and remote control television. VIP executive suites include balconies and parlors.

But at the Park Hyatt, luxury means more than fresh flowers and bathrobes. It denotes a standard of service that requires two employees for every guest. (The American hotel industry standard is 0.75 employees per guest.)

The Park Hyatt's high standards apparently appeal to both staff and guests. The hotel experiences virtually none of the high employee turnover that plagues much of the industry.

"Most of the original employees are still on the staff," says Paul Limbert, the hotel's general manager, who has headed the Park Hyatt's staff since the hotel opened in August 1986. "Some of our regular guests request rooms on a specific floor because they like the housekeepers there.

"But all of our staff are friendly and attentive," says Limbert. "Those are qualities we look for when we hire them. And every Park Hyatt employee is taught to 'never say no' to a guest."

Limbert worked in Paris and London before coming to the United States more than 20 years ago. He worked at Washington's Jefferson and Ritz-Carlton (DuPont Circle) hotels before taking over the Park Hyatt.

"At the Park Hyatt, we never say no. We meet the guest's request. There are no exceptions. We never offer excuses. We charge for special services, but we move a wall, rehang chandeliers, refurnish a room, or do whatever

With its luxurious atmosphere and quality service, the Park Hyatt Hotel has become synonomous with excellence.

To ensure that every guest's visit is a special and memorable experience, the hotel's staff is diligent about maintaining the upkeep of every area because no detail is too small to go unnoticed.

else a guest may require."

Limbert is not exaggerating when he speaks about moving walls and rehanging chandeliers. One frequent guest requires the use of a special dining table in the presidential suite. When she arrives, the suite is remodeled to her specifications. Comedienne Lily Tomlin stayed at the Park Hyatt while performing at the Kennedy Center. She asked that her room be specially darkened and soundproofed. The staff also added a kitchen and two bedrooms to her suite.

A relative newcomer to the Washington

hotel scene, the Park Hyatt has already acquired an impressive reputation among the diplomatic community and the international business set. Hotel facilities include five executive conference rooms.

A full English-style "tea" is served daily in the lobby lounge. "It's the only authentic English tea in Washington," says the British-born Limbert. Its menu includes traditional delicacies: cucumber sandwiches, smoked salmon, tomato and brie, and scones served with clotted cream. A choice of teas is properly brewed from loose tea. Tea at the Park

Hyatt features a circulating palm reader Wednesday through Sunday.

Many of Washington's insiders prefer more traditional American meals. They know that Melrose, the extraordinary Park Hyatt restaurant, is among the top handful of restaurants in Washington and has appeared on several national lists of America's "best."

Melrose executive chef Kenneth Juran prides himself on helping to restore the dignity of hotel dining. Superb dining has long been an international tradition at the world's elite hotels. Though long in decline throughout America, Melrose is leading what it sees as a nationwide effort to restore the custom.

Juran worked at the Greenbrier and Hotel Pierre in New York before moving to Europe. He worked at Le Chantecler at the Negresco Hotel in Nice, and at the Hotel de Paris in Monte Carlo.

At Melrose, Juran specializes in innovative, artistically presented American cuisine relying on regional ingredients. Since he uses only fresh produce, the menu changes frequently. But perhaps a diner will have an opportunity to enjoy his Spinach Angel Hair with Fresh Maine Lobster, Mascarpone Cheese, Tomato, and Herbs. That is an appetizer, not an entree.

Or how about a delicious Radicchio, Lambs Lettuce, Chickory, Walnut, and Apple Salad with warm Sonoma Goat Cheese dressing? It is wonderful with the Roast Squab with Huckleberries and Spaghetti Squash, perhaps accompanied by the Grilled Asparagus with Tomato Vinaigrette.

Be warned: the desserts at Melrose will tempt the most determined dieter. Fortunately, they will also provide taste buds with memories that will outlast any ensuing pangs of guilt.

Live music accompanies dinner. And every seat features a window view of the fountain. Courtyard seating is available in season. Melrose is open for breakfast (6:30 - 11:00), lunch (11:30-2:30), and dinner (5:30 - 10:30 Sunday - Thursday, to midnight on Friday and Saturday). The full Melrose menu is available to guests for private, in-room dining at any time.

Always cognizant that international travelers must function on a 24-hour day, the Park Hyatt provides many services around the clock. That concept is new to Washington, but greatly appreciated by the Park Hyatt's clientele. (As another international courtesy, the concierge keeps a list of all languages spoken by different members of the Park Hyatt staff.)

The Park Hyatt is a multicultural institution. There are not many hotels in the world that maintain a kosher kitchen (the Park Hyatt offers Washington's only luxury hotel with a kosher kitchen) and distribute an Arabic newspaper in the lobby.

"It is not unusual for us to have guests from cultures in conflict," says Limbert. Whenever there is conflict anywhere in the world, everyone involved sends delegations to Washington. Sometimes, both sides will choose to stay with us."

In less violent times, superb luxury suites of the Park Hyatt attract the chairmen of the boards of major multinational corporations, and diplomats from around the world. Senior corporate executives, entrepreneurs, high-ranking lobbyists, and members of trade delegations also favor the hotel.

The hotel's mezzanine-level business center operates daily, 8:00 - 5:00, providing word processing, desktop publishing support, and meeting other requirements of business traveling.

The center provides rental computers, typewriters, and dictating equipment. Complete and confidential secretarial assistance is, of course, also available.

"Smaller luxury hotels like ours are designed to serve the more discriminating traveler who demands immediate services," says Limbert. "Our guests won't tolerate the lines and crowds of the giant convention hotels. They are used to the standards set by European luxury hotels. They expect flawless service and total attention to every detail."

Park Hyatt guests for meetings and conventions receive the benefits of those standards. They too enjoy having their rooms serviced three times a day, fresh fruit served daily in their rooms, and a buffet luncheon served in the lounge.

Association executives will discover the benefits of a marketing program designed to service international travel agencies. It is a highly personalized program that includes meetings with the executive director and, when appropriate, his senior managers.

"We work with travel agencies from around the world," says Limbert. "We build long-term relationships. In the travel business, that means that we have to build trust. The agents may be 12,000 miles away, but they have to trust us with their best clients. They have learned that the Park Hyatt is highly reliable, that we always deliver exactly what we promise." Association executives and convention planners can expect the same quality of service and reliability. So too, can people planning special events. Recently, the Park Hyatt has emerged as a leading Washington hotel for special social and cultural events.

At such times, the hotel's lobbies and lounges become part of the club floor. Facilities include the 14,000-square-foot Ballroom, the 2,000-square-foot Hyde Park Room, and the 1,320-square-foot Tivoli Room. The hotel can handle 750 guests for a speech, 600 for a buffet reception, or provide dinner seating for up to 400 guests.

In addition to weddings, bar mitzvahs, and other private parties, the Park Hyatt hosts some of Washington's most popular social and cultural events. Highlights of the annual calendar include parties for the Folger Library, the Washington Opera Company, and the Washington Ballet.

Catering for all parties at the Park Hyatt is provided by Melrose, and most feature another look at that dessert menu. A couple of extra laps in the hotel pool, or a work-out in the health club, will make up for that moment of weakness. Maybe the Angel Food Cake with Red Wine Raspberry Sauce, or the Frozen Grand Marnier Souffle?

The lavish presidential suite features several amenities including a grand piano.

TRAVELOGUE, INC.

M. Osman Siddique, president and chief executive officer of Travelogue, Inc.

"Travel should be a pleasure, not an ordeal," says M. Osman Siddique, president of Travelogue, Inc., a locally owned and operated travel agency headquartered in downtown Washington. "It's an exciting activity and a dynamic profession. It should always be enjoyable, both for us and for our clients."

Siddique founded Travelogue in 1976, shortly after completing his MBA at Indiana University. From the start, his company has sought to satisfy the often conflicting demands of travelers and travel administrators.

The programs offered by this unique agency reflect its founder's creative thinking and desire to provide superior travel products and services. Travelogue's policies also reflect client needs for efficient, cost-effective travel.

Travel administrators demand the lowest costs and the most efficient financial reporting programs. So Travelogue uses an international computer network to cut through the maze of rates and special programs offered by suppliers around the world. The company provides financial reports that are custom-designed to client specifications, audit services for cost-reimbursable government contractors, and a "least-cost" guarantee.

But individual travelers rarely care about such technical considerations. They want top-quality, expert, personalized service. Travelogue's highly trained and closely supervised staff is honed to provide just that.

"We base our service expectations on international standards that our customers are familiar with and demand," says Siddique. A cordial executive, his gracious smiles complement his eye for detail and demanding requirements. Despite the company's rapid growth, Siddique remains in touch with daily operations.

The company's other officers are also intimately familiar with world-class service standards. Harvey Mikhail, Travelogue's executive vice president, is in charge of the overall running of the company. Mikhail holds a B.A. from Cairo University. Before joining Travelogue he accumulated 25 years of experience in airline marketing and travel agency management; in his last position he was the national account manager for one of the nation's largest travel management companies. His intelligence and quixotic spirit make themselves evident in his open, exuberant approach to travel marketing and customer service.

"Many of our customers are experienced world travelers. They know about the places that provide the 'best'—the spontaneous smiles, sincere respect, and deep-seated, instinctive concern—from first-hand experience," says Mikhail.

"They know the difference between efficiency, which has to do with making things work, and personalized service, which has to do with hospitality. That is precisely what we seek to provide—efficiency and hospitality."

Janet Penn, the company's vice president for operations and corporate service, also brings extensive travel industry experience to the company. She's a veteran of more than 15 years as a travel professional including regional manager for a national travel company and service consultant for a major travel computer company. Prior to her career in travel, she was an English teacher in a high school outside Washington, D.C.

Travelogue chooses people who have made a career commitment to the travel industry and to professional excellence. "Our consultants and transportation management staff are the best in the business," says Penn. "They come to Travelogue because they like the way we treat our clients and the way we treat our staff." As a result, Travelogue experiences minimal employee turnover and is proud of long-term, sustained client relationships.

A key component of such relationships is Travelogue's prized Executive Travel Program. Provided as part of a comprehensive association or corporate contract, the program is designed to meet the needs of senior executives and officers who travel frequently.

"We provide all our clients' senior executives with the kind of service that the big, national agencies provide only to the heads of *Fortune* 500 companies," says Siddique.

"For hard-driving, top-level professional travelers, luxury is a necessity that they are willing and able to pay for; nonetheless we want to make the experiences of our leisure travelers and budget business travelers as luxurious and pleasant as possible, too."

"We understand corporate travel policies

Above: Travelogue, Inc., Corporate Headquarters.

Left: Atrium, Travelogue, Inc., Corporate Headquarters building.

the travel industry felt the impact."

"We never allow the quality of overall services to suffer," says Mikhail. "That includes services provided by our suppliers as well as those we offer ourselves. Travelogue's suppliers are very aware of the level of services that we expect for our clients. This is a major reason our business continues to grow even during times when the overall market is weak."

Continued growth has allowed Travelogue to expand its staff to more than 60 employees, with offices in Fairfax,

and personal travel budgets," says Mikhail. "Travelogue's goal is to provide the best travel package—including the best agency service anywhere—no matter how much money the client has to spend. We train our people to sell the best values in travel and anticipate and avoid any possible pitfall that could occur."

Travelogue's policies have facilitated continued growth despite shrinking corporate budgets and other stresses of the early 1990s.

"It's no secret that travel has become highly competitive," says Siddique. "The overall volume of business and leisure travel dropped significantly at the start of the Gulf War and was slow to recover. Everybody in

Bethesda, Arlington, and Washington. Travelogue is the region's exclusive member of CORP-NET, a rapidly growing national network of privately held travel management companies.

Travelogue plans include continuing to diversify its product base. It is revamping its convention and meeting services, already among the most successful in the region. There are also plans to create a new division that will offer worldwide "special interest" tours such as trekking in the Andes, safaris in Africa, and bicycle tours in the Himalayas.

"Travel should be fun and exciting. We all love it. That's why we continue to grow as a travel management firm," says Mikhail.

GEORGETOWN SUITES

Living room of a one-bedroom suite.

Located in the heart of Georgetown, Georgetown Suites (1111 30th Street, N.W.) is surrounded by a shopper's paradise of boutiques, restaurants, and grocery stores. Minutes away from National Airport, the White House, and the commercial heart of Washington, the area offers easy access to public transportation and cruising taxicabs.

It is a location where you would expect to find an expensive, luxurious, upscale establishment. Instead, Georgetown Suites offers tourists and business professionals a reasonably priced alternative form of temporary quarters. Innovative, attractive, and beautifully maintained, this residential hotel provides a successful solution to the problem of finding affordable temporary housing. Georgetown Suites offers furnished studios, one-bedroom suites, and two-bedroom suites. Nightly rates are available, but most guests take advantage of the facilities for longer visits. Many stay for several weeks. A few stay several months. Several of the hotel's regular commercial tenants have even retained their units at Georgetown Suites for years.

Many corporations have discovered Georgetown Suites; they use its facilities whenever they have need of a short-term Washington office, or of housing for a sales team, legal group, or others on temporary assignment. The complex is also popular among state department employees, a group

that frequently has need of temporary housing in Washington.

While Georgetown Suites accepts nightly guests (about half the guests may stay for only a day or two), it is not a traditional hotel. For one thing, guests pay when they leave. (Under district law, guests signing in for three months or more save sales tax and occupancy tax.)

Many find that even the diverse, delectable delicacies of Georgetown's restaurants may eventually pale. Preparing one's own breakfast or dinner may occasionally become the most tempting choice. Such an economy also offers a creative approach to stretching limited government and corporate per diem expense payments.

Each suite at Georgetown Suites has a fully equipped kitchen including a full-size refrigerator with ice maker, a microwave, and a dishwasher. Dishes and flatware are provided along with basic cooking utensils and a list of neighborhood grocery stores. Linens and towels are furnished in all of the suites.

Full housekeeping services are available for all nightly and weekly reservations, and as an extra-cost option for extended stays. A complimentary continental breakfast is served to nightly guests. Unlimited local telephone service is included in the base rates for all units, and long distance calling is available with a credit card. Parking for guests' automobiles is provided as an extra fee option.

Georgetown Suites opened in January 1980, just in time for the inauguration of President Ronald Reagan. The building was originally planned for unfurnished apartments. Faced with growing competition, its owners, Jack Y. Matthews and William L. Walde, decided instead to offer a new form of temporary residence.

At first they offered their furnished units only on a month to month basis. Their concept soon proved itself to be an immediate success. Newly appointed White House staffers and several cabinet officers quickly made the Georgetown Suites an off-campus power center, AT&T became Georgetown Suites first corporate tenant, renting several units for use by visiting executives.

To manage their new facility, the owners recruited Joan Carroll as general manager. An opera singer with an illustrious European career, Carroll had returned to the United States following her retirement from the stage. She signed on with Georgetown Suites when it opened and has manged it since.

Nightly rates at Georgetown Suites are highly competitive with traditional hotels in the area. Long-term rates are about half the cost of nightly stays.

Georgetown Suites offers 134 furnished units, including several luxurious townhouses. Since they provide sufficient space for combined residential and office use, the townhouses are especially popular with corporate clients.

Just a few steps away from the C&O Canal.

Perhaps most tempting of all, the relaxation and beauty of the historic C&O Canal is just a few steps away. To a harried Washington newcomer, an evening walk along the canal's towpath may prove even more pleasurable than an invitation to the White House

Studio suite with kitchen facilities.

OMEGA WORLD TRAVEL

Above: Gloria Bohan, founder and president of Omega World Travel.

Right: Omega World Travel has become one of the U.S. travel industry's giants.

Gloria Bohan founded Omega World Travel in 1972. An expatriate New Yorker, she first came to Washington as an English teacher. But a wedding reception and honeymoon aboard the QE2 had introduced her to the travel industry and sparked her enthusiasm for a career in travel. It was on a whim and luck that this Washington success story was born.

Bohan's first office was in Fredericksburg, Virginia. Today the firm has more than 190 offices and 690 employees based throughout the nation. With annual sales topping $303 million, Omega World Travel has become one of the U.S. travel industry's giants. Omega is the largest woman-owned business

needs enthusiasm and motivation. They need to present a positive attitude."

All of these techniques are taught at the Omega Travel School, a program that was created to train Omega agents but is now open to the public. "Anybody can make a telephone call," explains Bohan. "Travel agents are necessary only as long as they provide services or amenities that aren't available elsewhere."

For its corporate travel programs, Omega provides extensive record-keeping and expense-tracking services. For personal and business travelers, the firm concentrates on expertise about locations, prices, and products.

It all comes wrapped in personal service.

in the Washington, D.C., area.

"You've got to be responsive to opportunity," says Bohan. "We feature small offices located close to customers' businesses. We provide one-on-one service. We customize everything we do. Our corporate culture is understanding the corporate cultures of our customers."

Bohan built the business with only a handful of hard-working employees. "We were all salesmen," she recalls. "I didn't have a 'salesman' working for me until about 1983. She is still her own best salesperson, spending the greater part of her time speaking to customers and potential accounts and touring the country on behalf of her business.

"Meeting people is what this business is all about. Everyone who works at Omega is a 'salesman.' All of my people know that. Everyone who deals directly with customers

Omega has no remote reservations centers. The individual agent follows each ticket from the time a reservation is made to the time the client returns from the trip. The same agents even routinely make personal follow-up calls, checking on how their clients' trips went.

"We've centralized our administration and decentralized our sales," says Bohan. "Our network of branch offices allows close personal contact with the travelers. Close personal contact with your clients is what this business is all about.

"Agencies must innovate to survive," continues Bohan. "There are about 29,000 travel agencies in the United States. That's a lot of competition."

There may be a lot of competition, but in the Washington market, and throughout the United States, Omega is clearly one of the big winners.

ACKNOWLEDGMENTS

Knowing that a writer is only as good as her editor, I am particularly grateful to Teri Davis Greenberg for her fine eye, patient ear, and valued ideas; and to my friend and colleague Sara Ketchum Piccini for her guidance at a critical stage in the manuscript. My special thanks also to Sidney O. Dewberry of Dewberry and Davis for sharing his encyclopedic, first-hand knowledge of the growth and development of the capital region and to Douglas M. Kleine of Professional Association Services for his wise analysis of social and political changes that have accompanied that growth. Many others also gave freely of their time, resources, and insight, including Winfield Kelly, Secretary of State of Maryland; Glenn Davidson of Arlington, press secretary to Virginia Governor L. Douglas Wilder; C. James Dowden of Mitchellville, Maryland; Robert Atkinson, Arlington County Business Conservation Program; Sara Amy Leach, Arlington Historical Alliance; Joseph Cater, Ph.D., Montgomery County Office of Economic Development; Jim Jones, of the law firm of Arnold & Porter and the Greater Washington Board of Trade; Yvonne Carignan, Lloyd House Library, City of Alexandria; Phil Hayward, *New Dominion* magazine; as well as countless librarians, historians, and helpful employees of government agencies throughout the region. Thanks to them all and to Edgar, Rocky, Power, A.G., and Paws and to my parents, Franklin and Virginia Jacob, for their continued encouragement.

Photo by Joseph Sohm/Chromosohm

BIBLIOGRAPHY

Books

Applewhite, E.J. *Washington Itself.* New York: Alfred A. Knopf, 1989.

Dickens, Charles. *American Notes, 1843.* New York: Books, Inc., n.d.

Fitzpatrick, Sandra and Maria R. Goodwin. *The Guide to Black Washington.* New York: Hippocrene Books, 1990.

Green, Constance McLaughlin. *Washington: A History of the Capital, 1800-1950.* Princeton: Princeton University Press, 1962.

Hagemann, James. *The Heritage of Virginia: The Story of Place James in the Old Dominion.* Norfolk: The Donning Company, 1986.

Harvey, Karen G. and Ross Stansfield. *Alexandria, A Pictorial History.* Norfolk: The Donning Company, 1977.

Hume, Ivor Noel. *Here Lies Virginia: An Archaeologist's View of Colonial Life and History.* New York: Alfred A. Knopf, 1963.

Jacob, Bonnie. *VIP Washington.* Laporte, PA: Great Destinations, 1991.

Jefferson, Thomas. *Notes on the State of Virginia (1787). New York: W.W. Norton & Company, 1954, 1972.*

Junior League of Washington. *An Illustrated History of the City of Washington.* New York: Alfred A. Knopf, 1985.

Netherton, Nan. *Clifton: Brigadoon in America.* Clifton, VA: Clifton Betterment Association, 1980.

Netherton, Nan and Ross. *Arlington County in Virginia: A Pictorial History.* Norfolk & Virginia Beach: The Donning Company, 1987.

Netherton, Nan and D. Sweig, J. Artemel, P. Hickin, and P. Reed. *Fairfax County, Virginia: A History.* Fairfax County Board of Supervisors, 1978.

Smith, Kathryn Schneider (ed.). *Washington at Home.* Northridge, CA: Windsor Publications, 1988.

Smithsonian Institution Press. *Official Guide to the Smithsonian.* Washington, D.C.: 1986.

Sprouse, Edith Moore. *Colchester: Colonial Port on the Potomac.* Fairfax, VA: Fairfax County Office of Comprehensive Planning, 1975.

Steadman, Melvin Lee. *Falls Church by Fence and Fireside.* Falls Church, VA: Falls Church Public Library, 1964.

Sween, Jane C. *Montgomery County: Two Centuries of Change.* Woodland Hills, CA: Windsor Publications, 1984.

Thane, Elswyth. *Mount Vernon is Ours.* New York: Duell, Sloan and Pearce, 1966.

Newspapers

Connection Newspapers, The Great Falls-McLean Sun Gazette Journal Newspapers, The Washington Post, The

Magazines

New Dominion Regardie's Washingtonian, The Washington Flyer

Miscellaneous Publications

Annandale Chamber of Commerce. *Community Guide to Annandale, Virginia,* 1989

City of Fairfax. *City of Fairfax Community Handbook.* (July 1989)

City of Fairfax. "Comprehensive Plan of the City of Fairfax, VA" (adopted November 29, 1988)

Fairfax County, VA, Office of Comprehensive Planning. *1989 Annual Report on the Environment,* Environmental Quality Advisory Council

Fairfax County Economic Development Authority. *Fairfax Prospectus:* Vol. 20, No. 1, "The Aerospace and Aviation Industry in Fairfax County" (February 1989); Vol. 20, No. 2, "Women and Minority Business Executives: A Key Part of Fairfax County's Success," (August 1989); Vol. 20, No. 3, "Computer Services in Fairfax County" (November 1989; Vol. 20, No. 1, "Business and Education: A Growing Partnership (1990)

Fairfax County Economic Development Authority Business Report: Annandale-Bailey's Crossroads-Seven Corners Area Market Report" (winter 1990); "Merrifield Area Market Report" (summer 1989); "1988-1989 Transportation Report" (December 1988); "Reston-Herndon Area Market Report" (summer 1988); "Southeast Fairfax Area Market Report" (summer 1990); "Springfield-Newington Area Market Report" (fall 1989); "Tyson's Corner Area Market Report" (summer 1988); "Yearend 1989 Real Estate and Market Review and 1989 Hotel Report (March 1990)

Fairfax County Office of Public Affairs. *Fairfax County Citizens Handbook, 1990-1991* (September 1990)

Fairfax County Office of Research and Statistics: "Demographic Profiles of Planning Districts, 1988 Household Survey Data" (May 1989); "1989 Fairfax County Profile" (1989)

Fairfax County Office of Research and Statistics, Research and Analysis Branch. "Demographic Profiles of Selected Communities in Fairfax County, VA" (March 1989)

Northern Virginia District Planning Commission: "Northern Virginia Demographic Trends, Working Paper No. 1" (November 1, 1989); "The New Northern Virginians" (1985)

Additional Resources

CITY, COUNTY, AND REGIONAL GOVERNMENTS AND COUNCILS

Alexandria, VA; Arlington County, VA; Bowie, MD; Fairfax, VA; Fairfax County, VA; Falls Church, VA; Gaithersburg, MD; Hyattsville, MD; Laurel, MD; Metropolitan Washington Area Council of Governments; Montgomery County, MD; Prince George's County, MD; Rockville, MD; Takoma Park, MD

ECONOMIC DEVELOPMENT OFFICES AND BOARDS OF TRADE

Alexandria Office of Economic Development; Arlington County Office of Economic Development; Fairfax County Office of Economic Development; Greater Washington Board of Trade; Maryland Office of Economic and Community Development; Montgomery County Office of Economic Development; Prince George's County Office of Economic Development

FEDERAL AGENCIES

U.S. Bureau of the Census; U.S. National Park Service

HISTORICAL SOCIETIES AND ORGANIZATIONS

Arlington County Historical Society; Fairfax County Historical Society; Historic Alexandria; Montgomery County Historical Society

LIBRARIES AND ARCHIVES

Library of Congress; Lloyd House Library, City of Alexandria, VA; Martin Luther King Library (District of Columbia), Washingtoniana Collection; National Archives

PLANNING AUTHORITIES AND REGIONAL ASSOCIATIONS

National Capital Area Park and Planning Authority; Northern Virginian Planning District Commission; Washington/Baltimore Regional Association

DIRECTORY OF CORPORATE SPONSORS

B & B Washington's Caterer, 180
7041 Blair Road Northwest
Washington, DC 20012
202/829-8640

CACI, 152
1100 North Glebe Road
Arlington, VA 22201
703/841-7800

Crestar Bank, 132
410 Pine Street
Vienna, VA 22180
703/242-2625

Design Cuisine, 173
2659 South Arlington Road
Arlington, VA 22206
703/979-9400

EDS, 160
13600 EDS Drive
Herndon, VA 22071
703/742-2000

Epstein Becker & Green, 140
1227 25th Street
Seventh Floor
Washington, DC 20037
202/861-0900

Fairchild Corporation, 154
300 West Service Road
Chantilly, VA 22201
703/478-5712

Fairfax Hospital, 178
3300 Gallows Road
Falls Church, VA 22046
703/698-1110

Freddie Mac, 134
8200 Jones Branch Drive
McLean, VA 22102
703/903-2550

Georgetown Suites, 188
1111 30th Street Northwest
Washington, DC 20007
202/298-7731

Thomas Havey & Company, 130
900 17th Street Northwest
Washington, DC 20006
202/331-9880

Howrey & Simon, 142
1730 Pennsylvania Avenue Northwest
Washington, DC 20006
202/783-0800

IBM Sterling, 168
1301 K Street Northwest
Washington, DC 20005
202/515-4602

Jones, Day, Reavis & Pogue, 131
1450 G Street Northwest
Washington, DC 20005
202/879-3939

The Journal Newspapers, 124
6883 Commercial Drive
Springfield, VA 22159
703/750-8012

Marymount University, 172
2807 North Globe Road
Arlington, VA 22207
703/284-1647

Maxima Corporation, 157
2101 East Jefferson Street
Rockville, MD 20852
301/230-2000

McGuire, Woods, Battle & Boothe, 133
8280 Greensboro Drive
Suite 900
McLean, VA 22102
703/712-5000

Media General Cable of Fairfax, 120
14650 Lee Road
Chantilly, VA 22021
703/378-8400

National Association of Life Underwriters, 138
1922 F Street Northwest
Washington, DC 20006
202/331-6001